21 Lessons

What I've Learned from Falling Down the Bitcoin Rabbit Hole

Gigi

21 Lessons
What I've Learned From Falling Down the Bitcoin Rabbit Hole
First edition. Version 0.3.11, git commit 6a933bb.

Copyright ©2018–2019 Gigi / @dergigi / dergigi.com

This book and its online version are distributed under the terms of the Creative Commons Attribution-ShareAlike 4.0 license. A reference copy of this license may be found at the official creative commons page.[a]

---

[a]https://creativecommons.org/licenses/by-sa/4.0

Dedicated to my wife, my child, and all the children of this world. May bitcoin serve you well, and provide a vision for a future worth fighting for.

Foreword

Some call it a religious experience. Others call it Bitcoin.

I first met Gigi in one of my spiritual homes – Riga, Latvia – the home of *The Baltic Honeybadger* Conference, where the most fervent of the Bitcoin faithful make a yearly pilgrimage. After a deep lunchtime conversation, the bond Gigi and I forged was as set in stone as a Bitcoin transaction that was processed when we first shook hands a few hours prior.

My other spiritual home, Christ Church, Oxford, where I had the privilege to study for my MBA, was where I had my "Rabbit Hole" moment. Like Gigi, I transcended the economic, technical and social realms, and was spiritually enveloped by Bitcoin. After "buying high" in the November 2013 bubble, there were several extremely hard-learned lessons to be had in the relentlessly crushing and seemingly never-ending 3-year bear market. These 21 Lessons would indeed have served me very well in that time. Many of these lessons are simply natural truths that, to the uninitiated, are obscured by an opaque, fragile film. By the end of this book however, the façade will fragment fiercely.

On a crystal-clear night in Oxford in late-August 2016, just a few weeks after the knife twisted in my heart again when the Bitfinex Exchange was hacked, I sat in quiet contemplation at Christ Church's Master's Garden. Times were tough, and I was at my mental and emotional breaking-point after what seemed to be a lifetime of torture; not because of financial loss, but of the crushing spiritual loss I felt being isolated in my world view. If only there were resources like this one at the time to see that I was not alone. The Master's Garden is a very special place to me and many who came before me over the centuries. It was there where one Charles Dodgson, a Math Tutor at Christ Church, observed one of his young pupils, Alice Liddell, the daughter of the Dean of Christ Church. Dodgson, better known by his pen-name, Lewis Carroll, used Alice and The Garden as his inspiration, and in the magic of that hallowed turf, I stared deeply into the crypto-chasm, and it stared blazingly back, annihilating my arrogance, and slapping my self-pride square in the face. I was finally at peace.

21 Lessons takes you on a true Bitcoin journey; not just a journey of philosophy, technology and economics, but of the soul.

As you dive deeper into the philosophy tersely laid out in 7 of the 21 Lessons, one can go as far as to understand the origin of all beings with enough time and contemplation. His 7 lessons on economics captures, in simple terms, how we are at the financial mercy of a small group of Mad Hatters, and how they have successfully managed to put blinders on our minds, hearts and souls. The 7 lessons on technology lay out the beauty and technologically-Darwinian perfection of Bitcoin. Being a non-technical Bitcoiner, the lessons provide a salient review of the underlying technological nature of Bitcoin, and indeed, the nature of technology itself.

In this transient experience we call life, we live, love and learn. But what is life but a timestamped order of events?

Conquering the Bitcoin mountain is not easy. False summits are rife, rocks are rough, and cracks and crevices are ubiquitously lying in wait to swallow you up. After reading this book, you will see that Gigi is the ultimate Bitcoin Sherpa, and I will appreciate him forever.

Hass McCook
November 29, 2019

"Would you tell me, please, which way I ought to go from here?"

"That depends a good deal on where you want to get to."

"I don't much care where –"

"Then it doesn't matter which way you go."

– Lewis Carroll, *Alice in Wonderland*

Contents

I. Philosophy   9

1. Immutability and Change   15
2. The Scarcity of Scarcity   19
3. Replication and Locality   21
4. The Problem of Identity   23
5. An Immaculate Conception   25
6. The Power of Free Speech   27
7. The Limits of Knowledge   29

II. Economics   31

8. Financial Ignorance   35
9. Inflation   39
10. Value   45
11. Money   47
12. The History and Downfall of Money   51

13. Fractional Reserve Insanity	59
14. Sound Money	65

III. Technology   73

15. Strength in Numbers	77
16. Reflections on "Don't Trust, Verify"	85
17. Telling Time Takes Work	93
18. Move Slowly and Don't Break Things	97
19. Privacy is Not Dead	101
20. Cypherpunks Write Code	103
21. Metaphors for Bitcoin's Future	107

Final Thoughts   115

About This Book
(... and About the Author)

This is a bit of an unusual book. But hey, Bitcoin is a bit of an unusual technology, so an unusual book about Bitcoin might be fitting. I'm not sure if I'm an unusual guy (I like to think of myself as a *regular* guy) but the story of how this book came to be, and how I came to be an author, is worth telling.

First of all, I'm not an author. I'm an engineer. I didn't study writing. I studied code and coding. Second of all, I never intended to write a book, let alone a book about Bitcoin. Hell, I'm not even a native speaker.[1] I'm just a guy who caught the Bitcoin bug. Hard.

Who am *I* to write a book about Bitcoin? That's a good question. The short answer is easy: I'm Gigi, and I'm a bitcoiner.

The long answer is a bit more nuanced.

My background is in computer science and software development. In a previous life, I was part of a research group that tried to make computers think and reason, among other things. In yet another previous life I wrote software for automated passport processing and related stuff which is even scarier. I know a thing or two about computers and our networked world, so I guess I have a bit of a head-start to understand the technical side of Bitcoin. However, as I try to outline in this book, the

---

[1]The reason why I'm writing these words in English is that my brain works in mysterious ways. Whenever something technical comes up, it switches to English mode.

tech side of things is only a tiny sliver of the beast which is Bitcoin. And every single one of these slivers is important.

This book came to be because of one simple question: *"What have you learned from Bitcoin?"* I tried to answer this question in a single tweet. Then the tweet turned into a tweetstorm. The tweetstorm turned into an article. The article turned into three articles. Three articles turned into 21 Lessons. And 21 Lessons turned into this book. So I guess I'm just really bad at condensing my thoughts into a single tweet.

"Why write this book?", you might ask. Again, there is a short and a long answer. The short answer is that I simply had to. I was (and still am) *possessed* by Bitcoin. I find it to be endlessly fascinating. I can't seem to stop thinking about it and the implications it will have on our global society. The long answer is that I believe that Bitcoin is the single most important invention of our time, and more people need to understand the nature of this invention. Bitcoin is still one of the most misunderstood phenomena of our modern world, and it took me years to fully realize the gravitas of this alien technology. Realizing what Bitcoin is and how it will transform our society is a profound experience. I hope to plant the seeds which might lead to this realization in your head.

While this section is titled *"About This Book (... and About the Author)"*, in the grand scheme of things, this book, who I am, and what I did doesn't really matter. I am just a node in the network, both literally *and* figuratively. Plus, you shouldn't trust what I'm saying anyway. As we bitcoiners like to say: do your own research, and most importantly: don't trust, verify.

I did my best to do my homework and provide plenty of sources for you, dear reader, to dive into. In addition to the footnotes and citations in this book, I try to keep an updated list of resources at 21lessons.com/rabbithole and on bitcoin-resources.com, which also lists plenty of other curated resources, books, and podcasts that will help you to understand what Bitcoin is.

In short, this is simply a book about Bitcoin, written by a bitcoiner. Bitcoin doesn't need this book, and you probably don't need this book to understand Bitcoin. I believe that Bitcoin will be understood by you as soon as *you* are ready, and I also believe that the first fractions of a bitcoin will find you as soon as you are ready to receive them. In essence, everyone will get ₿itcoin at exactly the right time. In the meanwhile, Bitcoin simply is, and that is enough.[2]

---

[2]Beautyon, *Bitcoin is. And that is enough.* [8]

Preface

Falling down the Bitcoin rabbit hole is a strange experience. Like many others, I feel like I have learned more in the last couple of years studying Bitcoin than I have during two decades of formal education.

The following lessons are a distillation of what I've learned. First published as an article series titled *"What I've Learned From Bitcoin,"* what follows can be seen as a third edition of the original series.

Like Bitcoin, these lessons aren't a static thing. I plan to work on them periodically, releasing updated versions and additional material in the future.

Unlike Bitcoin, future versions of this project do not have to be backward compatible. Some lessons might be extended, others might be reworked or replaced.

Bitcoin is an inexhaustible teacher, which is why I do not claim that these lessons are all-encompassing or complete. They are a reflection of my personal journey down the rabbit hole. There are many more lessons to be learned, and every person will learn something different from entering the world of Bitcoin.

I hope that you will find these lessons useful and that the process of learning them by reading won't be as arduous and painful as learning them firsthand.

21 Lessons

"Oh, you foolish Alice!" she said again, "how can you learn lessons in here? Why, there's hardly room for you, and no room at all for any lesson-books!"

– Lewis Carroll, *Alice in Wonderland*

Introduction

> *"But I don't want to go among mad people,"*
> *Alice remarked. "Oh, you can't help that,"*
> *said the Cat: "we're all mad here. I'm mad.*
> *You're mad." "How do you know I'm mad?"*
> *said Alice. "You must be," said the Cat, "or*
> *you wouldn't have come here."*
>
> — Lewis Carroll, *Alice in Wonderland*

In October 2018, Arjun Balaji asked the innocuous question, *What have you learned from Bitcoin?* After trying to answer this question in a short tweet, and failing miserably, I realized that the things I've learned are far too numerous to answer quickly, if at all.

The things I've learned are, obviously, about Bitcoin - or at least related to it. However, while some of the inner workings of Bitcoin are explained, the following lessons are not an explanation of how Bitcoin works or what it is, they might, however, help to explore some of the things Bitcoin touches: philosophical questions, economic realities, and technological innovations.

The *21 Lessons* are structured in bundles of seven, resulting in three chapters. Each chapter looks at Bitcoin through a different lens, extracting what lessons can be learned by inspecting this strange network from a different angle.

Chapter 1 explores the philosophical teachings of Bitcoin. The interplay of immutability and change, the concept of true scarcity, Bitcoin's immaculate conception, the problem of identity, the contradiction of replication and locality, the power of free speech, and the limits of knowledge.

Chapter 2 explores the economic teachings of Bitcoin. Lessons about financial ignorance, inflation, value, money and the history of money, fractional reserve banking, and how Bitcoin is re-introducing sound money in a sly, roundabout way.

Chapter 3 explores some of the lessons learned by examining the technology of Bitcoin. Why there is strength in numbers, reflections on trust, why telling time takes work, how moving slowly and not breaking things is a feature and not a bug, what Bitcoin's creation can tell us about privacy, why cypherpunks write code (and not laws), and what metaphors might be useful to explore Bitcoin's future.

Each lesson contains several quotes and links throughout the text. If an idea is worth exploring in more detail, you can follow the links to related works in the footnotes or in the bibliography.

Even though some prior knowledge about Bitcoin is beneficial, I hope that these lessons can be digested by any curious reader. While some relate to each other, each lesson should be able to stand on its own and can be read independently. I did my best to shy away from technical jargon, even though some domain-specific vocabulary is unavoidable.

I hope that my writing serves as inspiration for others to dig beneath the surface and examine some of the deeper questions Bitcoin raises. My own inspiration came from a multitude of authors and content creators to all of whom I am eternally grateful.

Last but not least: my goal in writing this is not to convince you of anything. My goal is to make you think, and show you that there is way more to Bitcoin than meets the eye. I can't even tell you what Bitcoin is or what Bitcoin will teach you. You will have to find that out for yourself.

> "After this, there is no turning back. You take the blue pill — the story ends, you wake up in your bed and believe whatever you want to believe. You take the red pill[3] — you stay in Wonderland, and I show you how deep the rabbit hole goes."
>
> – Morpheus

---

[3] the *orange* pill

Remember: All I'm offering is the truth. Nothing more.

Part I.

Philosophy

Philosophy

> *The mouse looked at her rather inquisitively, and seemed to her to wink with one of its little eyes, but it said nothing.*
>
> – Lewis Carroll, *Alice in Wonderland*

Looking at Bitcoin superficially, one might conclude that it is slow, wasteful, unnecessarily redundant, and overly paranoid. Looking at Bitcoin inquisitively, one might find out that things are not as they seem at first glance.

Bitcoin has a way of taking your assumptions and turning them on their heads. After a while, just when you were about to get comfortable again, Bitcoin will smash through the wall like a bull in a china shop and shatter your assumptions once more.

Bitcoin is a child of many disciplines. Like blind monks examining an elephant, everyone who approaches this novel technology does so from a different angle. And everyone will come to different conclusions about the nature of the beast.

The following lessons are about some of my assumptions which Bitcoin shattered, and the conclusions I arrived at. Philosophical questions of immutability, scarcity, locality, and identity are explored in the first four lessons. Every part consists of seven lessons.

Part I – Philosophy:

1. Immutability and change
2. The scarcity of scarcity
3. Replication and locality
4. The problem of identity
5. An immaculate conception
6. The power of free speech
7. The limits of knowledge

Lesson 5 explores how Bitcoin's origin story is not only fascinating but absolutely essential for a leaderless system. The last two lessons of this chapter explore the power of free speech and the limits of our individual knowledge, reflected by the surprising depth of the Bitcoin rabbit hole.

I hope that you will find the world of Bitcoin as educational, fascinating and entertaining as I did and still do. I invite you to follow the white rabbit and explore the depths of this rabbit hole. Now hold on to your pocket watch, pop down, and enjoy the fall.

1. Immutability and Change

> *"I wonder if I've been changed in the night. Let me think. Was I the same when I got up this morning? I almost think I can remember feeling a little different. But if I'm not the same, the next question is 'Who in the world am I?' Ah, that's the great puzzle!"*
>
> – Alice

Bitcoin is inherently hard to describe. It is a *new thing*, and any attempt to draw a comparison to previous concepts – be it by calling it digital gold or the internet of money – is bound to fall short of the whole. Whatever your favorite analogy might be, two aspects of Bitcoin are absolutely essential: decentralization and immutability.

One way to think about Bitcoin is as an automated social contract[1]. The software is just one piece of the puzzle, and hoping to change Bitcoin by changing the software is an exercise in futility. One would have to convince the rest of the network to adopt the changes, which is more a psychological effort than a software engineering one.

The following might sound absurd at first, like so many other things in this space, but I believe that it is profoundly true nonetheless: You won't change Bitcoin, but Bitcoin will change you.

---

[1]Hasu, Unpacking Bitcoin's Social Contract [32]

15

> "Bitcoin will change us more than we will change it."
>
> – Marty Bent[2]

It took me a long time to realize the profundity of this. Since Bitcoin is just software and all of it is open-source, you can simply change things at will, right? Wrong. *Very* wrong. Unsurprisingly, Bitcoin's creator knew this all too well.

> "The nature of Bitcoin is such that once version 0.1 was released, the core design was set in stone for the rest of its lifetime."
>
> – Satoshi Nakamoto[3]

Many people have attempted to change Bitcoin's nature. So far all of them have failed. While there is an endless sea of forks and altcoins, the Bitcoin network still does its thing, just as it did when the first node went online. The altcoins won't matter in the long run. The forks will eventually starve to death. Bitcoin is what matters. As long as our fundamental understanding of mathematics and/or physics doesn't change, the Bitcoin honeybadger will continue to not care.

> "Bitcoin is the first example of a new form of life. It lives and breathes on the internet. It lives because it can pay people to keep it alive. [...] It can't be changed. It can't be argued with. It can't be tampered with. It can't be corrupted. It can't be stopped. [...] If nuclear war destroyed half of our planet, it would continue to live, uncorrupted."
>
> – Ralph Merkle[4]

---

[2]Tales From the Crypt [10]
[3]BitcoinTalk forum post: 'Re: Transactions and Scripts...' [56]
[4]DAOs, Democracy and Governance, [44]

The heartbeat of the Bitcoin network will outlast all of ours.

Realizing the above changed me way more than the past blocks of the Bitcoin blockchain ever will. It changed my time preference, my understanding of economics, my political views, and so much more. Hell, it is even changing people's diets[5]. If all of this sounds crazy to you, you're in good company. All of this is crazy, and yet it is happening.

Bitcoin taught me that it won't change. I will.

---

[5]Inside the World of the Bitcoin Carnivores, [58]

2. The Scarcity of Scarcity

> *"That's quite enough - I hope I sha'n't grow any more..."*
>
> – Alice

In general, the advance of technology seems to make things more abundant. More and more people are able to enjoy what previously have been luxurious goods. Soon, we will all live like kings. Most of us already do. As Peter Diamandis wrote in Abundance [23]: "Technology is a resource-liberating mechanism. It can make the once scarce the now abundant."

Bitcoin, an advanced technology in itself, breaks this trend and creates a new commodity which is truly scarce. Some even argue that it is one of the scarcest things in the universe. The supply can't be inflated, no matter how much effort one chooses to expend towards creating more.

> "Only two things are genuinely scarce: time and bitcoin."
>
> – Saifedean Ammous[1]

Paradoxically, it does so by a mechanism of copying. Transactions are broadcast, blocks are propagated, the distributed ledger is — well, you guessed it — distributed. All of these are just fancy words for copying. Heck, Bitcoin even copies itself onto as many computers as it can, by incentivizing individual people to run full nodes and mine new blocks.

All of this duplication wonderfully works together in a concerted effort to produce scarcity.

---

[1] Presentation on The Bitcoin Standard [2]

In a time of abundance, Bitcoin taught me what real scarcity is.

3. Replication and Locality

> *Next came an angry voice – the rabbit's –*
> *"Pat, Pat! where are you?"*
> – Lewis Carroll, *Alice in Wonderland*

Quantum mechanics aside, locality is a non-issue in the physical world. The question *"Where is X?"* can be answered in a meaningful way, no matter if X is a person or an object. In the digital world, the question of *where* is already a tricky one, but not impossible to answer. Where are your emails, really? A bad answer would be "the cloud", which is just someone else's computer. Still, if you wanted to track down every storage device which has your emails on it you could, in theory, locate them.

With bitcoin, the question of "where" is *really* tricky. Where, exactly, are your bitcoins?

> "I opened my eyes, looked around, and asked the inevitable, the traditional, the lamentably hackneyed postoperative question: 'Where am I?'"
>
> – Daniel Dennett[1]

The problem is twofold: First, the distributed ledger is distributed by full replication, meaning the ledger is everywhere. Second, there are no bitcoins. Not only physically, but *technically*.

Bitcoin keeps track of a set of unspent transaction outputs, without ever having to refer to an entity which represents a

---

[1] Daniel Dennett, *Where Am I?* [21]

bitcoin. The existence of a bitcoin is inferred by looking at the set of unspent transaction outputs and calling every entry with 100 million base units a bitcoin.

> "Where is it, at this moment, in transit? [...] First, there are no bitcoins. There just aren't. They don't exist. There are ledger entries in a ledger that's shared [...] They don't exist in any physical location. The ledger exists in every physical location, essentially. Geography doesn't make sense here — it is not going to help you figuring out your policy here."
>
> – Peter Van Valkenburgh[2]

So, what do you actually own when you say *"I have a bitcoin"* if there are no bitcoins? Well, remember all these strange words which you were forced to write down by the wallet you used? Turns out these magic words are what you own: a magic spell[3] which can be used to add some entries to the public ledger — the keys to "move" some bitcoins. This is why, for all intents and purposes, your private keys *are* your bitcoins. If you think I'm making all of this up feel free to send me your private keys.

Bitcoin taught me that locality is a tricky business.

---

[2]Peter Van Valkenburgh on the *What Bitcoin Did* podcast, episode 49 [73]
[3]The Magic Dust of Cryptography: How digital information is changing our society [30]

Figure 0.1.: Blind monks examining the Bitcoin bull

4. The Problem of Identity

"Who are you?" said the caterpillar.
— Lewis Carroll, *Alice in Wonderland*

Nic Carter, in an homage to Thomas Nagel's treatment of the same question in regards to a bat, wrote an excellent piece which discusses the following question: What is it like to be a bitcoin? He brilliantly shows that open, public blockchains in general, and Bitcoin in particular, suffer from the same conundrum as the ship of Theseus[1]: which Bitcoin is the real Bitcoin?

> "Consider just how little persistence Bitcoin's components have. The entire codebase has been reworked, altered, and expanded such that it barely resembles its original version. [...] The registry of who owns what, the ledger itself, is virtually the only persistent trait of the network [...] To be considered truly leaderless, you must surrender the easy solution of having an entity that can designate one chain as the legitimate one."
>
> — Nic Carter[2]

It seems like the advancement of technology keeps forcing us to take these philosophical questions seriously. Sooner or later, self-driving cars will be faced with real-world versions of the

---

[1] In the metaphysics of identity, the ship of Theseus is a thought experiment that raises the question of whether an object that has had all of its components replaced remains fundamentally the same object. [98]

[2] Nic Carter, *What is it like to be a bitcoin?* [19]

trolley problem, forcing them to make ethical decisions about whose lives do matter and whose do not.

Cryptocurrencies, especially since the first contentious hard-fork, force us to think about and agree upon the metaphysics of identity. Interestingly, the two biggest examples we have so far have lead to two different answers. On August 1, 2017, Bitcoin split into two camps. The market decided that the unaltered chain is the original Bitcoin. One year earlier, on October 25, 2016, Ethereum split into two camps. The market decided that the *altered* chain is the original Ethereum.

If properly decentralized, the questions posed by the *Ship of Theseus* will have to be answered in perpetuity for as long as these networks of value-transfer exist.

Bitcoin taught me that decentralization contradicts identity.

5. An Immaculate Conception

> *"Their heads are gone," the soldiers shouted in reply...*
> — Lewis Carroll, *Alice in Wonderland*

Everyone loves a good origin story. The origin story of Bitcoin is a fascinating one, and the details of it are more important than one might think at first. Who is Satoshi Nakamoto? Was he one person or a group of people? Was he a she? Time-traveling alien, or advanced AI? Outlandish theories aside, we will probably never know. And this is important.

Satoshi chose to be anonymous. He planted the seed of Bitcoin. He stuck around for long enough to make sure the network won't die in its infancy. And then he vanished.

What might look like a weird anonymity stunt is actually crucial for a truly decentralized system. No centralized control. No centralized authority. No inventor. No-one to prosecute, torture, blackmail, or extort. An immaculate conception of technology.

> "One of the greatest things that Satoshi did was disappear."
>
> — Jimmy Song[1]

---

[1] Jimmy Song, *Why Bitcoin is Different* [67]

Since the birth of Bitcoin, thousands of other cryptocurrencies were created. None of these clones share its origin story. If you want to supersede Bitcoin, you will have to transcend its origin story. In a war of ideas, narratives dictate survival.

> "Gold was first fashioned into jewelry and used for barter over 7,000 years ago. Gold's captivating gleam led to it being considered a gift from the gods."
>
> Austrian Mint[2]

Like gold in ancient times, Bitcoin might be considered a gift from the gods. Unlike gold, Bitcoins origins are all too human. And this time, we know who the gods of development and maintenance are: people all over the world, anonymous or not.

Bitcoin taught me that narratives are important.

---

[2]The Austrian Mint, *Gold: The Extraordinary Metal* [46]

6. The Power of Free Speech

> *"I beg your pardon?" said the mouse, frowning, but very politely, "did you speak?"*
> – Lewis Carroll, *Alice in Wonderland*

Bitcoin is an idea. An idea which, in its current form, is the manifestation of a machinery purely powered by text. Every aspect of Bitcoin is text: The whitepaper is text. The software which is run by its nodes is text. The ledger is text. Transactions are text. Public and private keys are text. Every aspect of Bitcoin is text, and thus equivalent to speech.

> "Congress shall make no law respecting an establishment of religion, or prohibiting the free exercise thereof; or abridging the freedom of speech, or of the press; or the right of the people peaceably to assemble, and to petition the Government for a redress of grievances."
>
> – First Amendment to the U.S. Constitution

Although the final battle of the Crypto Wars[1] has not been fought yet, it will be very difficult to criminalize an idea, let alone an idea which is based on the exchange of text messages. Every time a government tries to outlaw text or speech, we slip

---
[1] The *Crypto Wars* is an unofficial name for the U.S. and allied governments' attempts to undermine encryption. [26] [78]

down a path of absurdity which inevitably leads to abominations like illegal numbers[2] and illegal primes[3].

As long as there is a part of the world where speech is free as in *freedom*, Bitcoin is unstoppable.

> "There is no point in any Bitcoin transaction that Bitcoin ceases to be *text*. It is *all text*, all the time. [...] Bitcoin is *text*. Bitcoin is *speech*. It cannot be regulated in a free country like the USA with guaranteed inalienable rights and a First Amendment that explicitly excludes the act of publishing from government oversight."
>
> – Beautyon[4]

Bitcoin taught me that in a free society, free speech and free software are unstoppable.

---

[2] An illegal number is a number that represents information which is illegal to possess, utter, propagate, or otherwise transmit in some legal jurisdiction.[84]

[3] An illegal prime is a prime number that represents information whose possession or distribution is forbidden in some legal jurisdictions. One of the first illegal primes was found in 2001. When interpreted in a particular way, it describes a computer program that bypasses the digital rights management scheme used on DVDs. Distribution of such a program in the United States is illegal under the Digital Millennium Copyright Act. An illegal prime is a kind of illegal number.[85]

[4] Beautyon, *Why America can't regulate Bitcoin* [7]

7. The Limits of Knowledge

> *"Down, down, down. Would the fall never come to an end?"*
>
> – Lewis Carroll, *Alice in Wonderland*

Getting into Bitcoin is a humbling experience. I thought that I knew things. I thought that I was educated. I thought that I knew my computer science, at the very least. I studied it for years, so I have to know everything about digital signatures, hashes, encryption, operational security, and networks, right?

Wrong.

Learning all the fundamentals which make Bitcoin work is hard. Understanding all of them deeply is borderline impossible.

> *"No one has found the bottom of the Bitcoin rabbit hole."*
>
> – Jameson Lopp[1]

My list of books to read keeps expanding way quicker than I could possibly read them. The list of papers and articles to read is virtually endless. There are more podcasts on all of these topics than I could ever listen to. It truly is humbling. Further, Bitcoin is evolving and it's almost impossible to stay up-to-date with the accelerating rate of innovation. The dust of the first layer hasn't even settled yet, and people have already built the second layer and are working on the third.

---

[1] Jameson Lopp, tweet from Nov 11, 2018 [41]

Figure 7.1.: The Bitcoin rabbit hole is bottomless.

Bitcoin taught me that I know very little about almost anything. It taught me that this rabbit hole is bottomless.

Part II.

Economics

Economics

> *"A large rose tree stood near the entrance of the garden: the roses on it were white, but there were three gardeners at it, busily painting them red. This Alice thought a very curious thing..."*
>
> – Lewis Carroll, *Alice in Wonderland*

Money doesn't grow on trees. To believe that it does is foolish, and our parents make sure that we know about that by repeating this saying like a mantra. We are encouraged to use money wisely, to not spend it frivolously, and to save it in good times to help us through the bad. Money, after all, does not grow on trees.

Bitcoin taught me more about money than I ever thought I would need to know. Through it, I was forced to explore the history of money, banking, various schools of economic thought, and many other things. The quest to understand Bitcoin lead me down a plethora of paths, some of which I try to explore in this chapter.

In the first seven lessons some of the philosophical questions Bitcoin touches on were discussed. The next seven lessons will take a closer look at money and economics.

Part II – Economics:

8. Financial ignorance

9. Inflation

10. Value

11. Money

12. The history and downfall of money

13. Fractional reserve insanity

14. Sound money

Again, I will only be able to scratch the surface. Bitcoin is not only ambitious, but also broad and deep in scope, making it impossible to cover all relevant topics in a single lesson, essay, article, or book. I doubt if it is even possible at all.

Bitcoin is a new form of money, which makes learning about economics paramount to understanding it. Dealing with the nature of human action and the interactions of economic agents, economics is probably one of the largest and fuzziest pieces of the Bitcoin puzzle.

Again, these lessons are an exploration of the various things I have learned from Bitcoin. They are a personal reflection of my journey down the rabbit hole. Having no background in economics, I am definitely out of my comfort zone and especially aware that any understanding I might have is incomplete. I will do my best to outline what I have learned, even at the risk of making a fool out of myself. After all, I am still trying to answer the question: *"What have you learned from Bitcoin?"*

After seven lessons examined through the lens of philosophy, let's use the lens of economics to look at seven more. Economy class is all I can offer this time. Final destination: *sound money*.

8. Financial Ignorance

> *"And what an ignorant little girl she'll think me for asking! No, it'll never do to ask: perhaps I shall see it written up somewhere."*
> – Lewis Carroll, *Alice in Wonderland*

One of the most surprising things, to me, was the amount of finance, economics, and psychology required to get a grasp of what at first glance seems to be a purely *technical* system — a computer network. To paraphrase a little guy with hairy feet: "It's a dangerous business, Frodo, stepping into Bitcoin. You read the whitepaper, and if you don't keep your feet, there's no knowing where you might be swept off to."

To understand a new monetary system, you have to get acquainted with the old one. I began to realize very soon that the amount of financial education I enjoyed in the educational system was essentially *zero*.

Like a five-year-old, I began to ask myself a lot of questions: How does the banking system work? How does the stock market work? What is fiat money? What is *regular* money? Why is there so much debt?[1] How much money is actually printed, and who decides that?

---

[1] https://www.usdebtclock.org/

After a mild panic about the sheer scope of my ignorance, I found reassurance in realizing that I was in good company.

> "Isn't it ironic that Bitcoin has taught me more about money than all these years I've spent working for financial institutions? ...including starting my career at a central bank"
>
> – Aaron[2]

> "I've learned more about finance, economics, technology, cryptography, human psychology, politics, game theory, legislation, and myself in the last three months of crypto than the last three and a half years of college"
>
> – Dunny[3]

These are just two of the many confessions all over twitter.[4] Bitcoin, as was explored in Lesson 1, is a living thing. Mises argued that economics also is a living thing. And as we all know from personal experience, living things are inherently difficult to understand.

> "A scientific system is but one station in an endlessly progressing search for knowledge. It is necessarily affected by the insufficiency inherent in every human effort. But to acknowledge these facts does not mean that present-day economics is backward. It merely means that economics is a living thing — and to live implies both imperfection and change."
>
> – Ludwig von Mises[5]

---

[2]Aaron (`@aarontaycc`, `@fiatminimalist`), tweet from Dec. 12, 2018 [45]
[3]Dunny (`@BitcoinDunny`), tweet from Nov. 28, 2017 [24]
[4]See `http://bit.ly/btc-learned` for more confessions on twitter.
[5]Ludwig von Mises, *Human Action* [74]

We all read about various financial crises in the news, wonder about how these big bailouts work and are puzzled over the fact that no one ever seems to be held accountable for damages which are in the trillions. I am still puzzled, but at least I am starting to get a glimpse of what is going on in the world of finance.

Some people even go as far as to attribute the general ignorance on these topics to systemic, willful ignorance. While history, physics, biology, math, and languages are all part of our education, the world of money and finance surprisingly is only explored superficially, if at all. I wonder if people would still be willing to accrue as much debt as they currently do if everyone would be educated in personal finance and the workings of money and debt. Then I wonder how many layers of aluminum make an effective tinfoil hat. Probably three.

> "Those crashes, these bailouts, are not accidents. And neither is it an accident that there is no financial education in school. [...] It's premeditated. Just as prior to the Civil War it was illegal to educate a slave, we are not allowed to learn about money in school."
>
> – Robert Kiyosaki[6]

Like in The Wizard of Oz, we are told to pay no attention to the man behind the curtain. Unlike in The Wizard of Oz, we now have real wizardry[7]: a censorship-resistant, open, borderless network of value-transfer. There is no curtain, and the magic is visible to anyone.[8]

Bitcoin taught me to look behind the curtain and face my financial ignorance.

---
[6]Robert Kiyosaki, *Why the Rich are Getting Richer*[39]
[7]http://bit.ly/btc-wizardry
[8]https://github.com/bitcoin/bitcoin

9. Inflation

> *"My dear, here we must run as fast as we can, just to stay in place. And if you wish to go anywhere you must run twice as fast as that."*
> – The Queen of Hearts

Trying to understand monetary inflation, and how a non-inflationary system like Bitcoin might change how we do things, was the starting point of my venture into economics. I knew that inflation was the rate at which new money was created, but I didn't know too much beyond that.

While some economists argue that inflation is a good thing, others argue that "hard" money which can't be inflated easily — as we had in the days of the gold standard — is essential for a healthy economy. Bitcoin, having a fixed supply of 21 million, agrees with the latter camp.

Usually, the effects of inflation are not immediately obvious. Depending on the inflation rate (as well as other factors) the time between cause and effect can be several years. Not only that, but inflation affects different groups of people more than others. As Henry Hazlitt points out in *Economics in One Lesson*: "The art of economics consists in looking not merely at the immediate but at the longer effects of any act or policy; it consists in tracing the consequences of that policy not merely for one group but for all groups."

One of my personal lightbulb moments was the realization that issuing new currency — printing more money — is a *completely* different economic activity than all the other economic activities. While real goods and real services produce real value for real people, printing money effectively does the opposite: it takes away value from everyone who holds the currency which is being inflated.

> "Mere inflation — that is, the mere issuance of more money, with the consequence of higher wages and prices — may look like the creation of more demand. But in terms of the actual production and exchange of real things it is not."
>
> – Henry Hazlitt[1]

The destructive force of inflation becomes obvious as soon as a little inflation turns into *a lot*. If money hyperinflates things get ugly real quick.[2] As the inflating currency falls apart, it will fail to store value over time and people will rush to get their hands on any goods which might do.

Another consequence of hyperinflation is that all the money which people have saved over the course of their life will effectively vanish. The paper money in your wallet will still be there, of course. But it will be exactly that: worthless paper.

Money declines in value with so-called "mild" inflation as well. It just happens slowly enough that most people don't notice the diminishing of their purchasing power. And once the printing presses are running, currency can be easily inflated, and what used to be mild inflation might turn into a strong cup of inflation by the push of a button. As Friedrich Hayek pointed out in one of his essays, mild inflation usually leads to outright inflation.

---

[1] Henry Hazlitt, *Economics in One Lesson* [35]
[2] https://en.wikipedia.org/wiki/Hyperinflation [83]

Figure 9.1.: Hyperinflation in the Weimar Republic (1921-1923)

> "'Mild' steady inflation cannot help — it can lead only to outright inflation."
>
> – Friedrich Hayek[3]

Inflation is particularly devious since it favors those who are closer to the printing presses. It takes time for the newly created money to circulate and prices to adjust, so if you are able to get your hands on more money before everyone else's devaluates you are ahead of the inflationary curve. This is also why inflation can be seen as a hidden tax because in the end governments profit from it while everyone else ends up paying the price.

> "I do not think it is an exaggeration to say history is largely a history of inflation, and usually of inflations engineered by governments for the gain of governments."
>
> – Friedrich Hayek[4]

---

[3]Friedrich Hayek, *1980s Unemployment and the Unions* [33]
[4]Friedrich Hayek, *Good Money* [34]

So far, all government-controlled currencies have eventually been replaced or have collapsed completely. No matter how small the rate of inflation, "steady" growth is just another way of saying exponential growth. In nature as in economics, all systems which grow exponentially will eventually have to level off or suffer from catastrophic collapse.

"It can't happen in my country," is what you're probably thinking. You don't think that if you are from Venezuela, which is currently suffering from hyperinflation. With an inflation rate of over 1 million percent, money is basically worthless. [75]

It might not happen in the next couple of years, or to the particular currency used in your country. But a glance at the list of historical currencies[5] shows that it will inevitably happen over a long enough period of time. I remember and used plenty of those listed: the Austrian schilling, the German mark, the Italian lira, the French franc, the Irish pound, the Croatian dinar, etc. My grandma even used the Austro-Hungarian Krone. As time moves on, the currencies currently in use[6] will slowly but surely move to their respective graveyards. They will hyperinflate or be replaced. They will soon be historical currencies. We will make them obsolete.

> "History has shown that governments will inevitably succumb to the temptation of inflating the money supply."
>
> – Saifedean Ammous[7]

---

[5] See *List of historical currencies* on Wikipedia. [91]
[6] See *List of currencies* on Wikipedia [90]
[7] Saifedean Ammous, *The Bitcoin Standard* [1]

Why is Bitcoin different? In contrast to currencies mandated by the government, monetary goods which are not regulated by governments, but by the laws of physics[8], tend to survive and even hold their respective value over time. The best example of this so far is gold, which, as the aptly-named *Gold-to-Decent-Suit Ratio*[9] shows, is holding its value over hundreds and even thousands of years. It might not be perfectly "stable" — a questionable concept in the first place — but the value it holds will at least be in the same order of magnitude.

If a monetary good or currency holds its value well over time and space, it is considered to be *hard*. If it can't hold its value, because it easily deteriorates or inflates, it is considered a *soft* currency. The concept of hardness is essential to understand Bitcoin and is worthy of a more thorough examination. We will return to it in the last economic lesson: sound money.

As more and more countries suffer from hyperinflation more and more people will have to face the reality of hard and soft money. If we are lucky, maybe even some central bankers will be forced to re-evaluate their monetary policies. Whatever might happen, the insights I have gained thanks to Bitcoin will probably be invaluable, no matter the outcome.

Bitcoin taught me about the hidden tax of inflation and the catastrophe of hyperinflation.

---

[8]Gigi, *Bitcoin's Energy Consumption - A shift in perspective* [29]
[9]History shows that the price of an ounce of gold equals the price of a decent men's suit, according to Sionna investment managers [42]

10. Value

> "It was the white rabbit, trotting slowly back again, and looking anxiously about it as it went, as if it had lost something..."
> – Lewis Carroll, *Alice in Wonderland*

Value is somewhat paradoxical, and there are multiple theories[1] which try to explain why we value certain things over other things. People have been aware of this paradox for thousands of years. As Plato wrote in his dialogue with Euthydemus, we value some things because they are rare, and not merely based on their necessity for our survival.

> "And if you are prudent you will give this same counsel to your pupils also — that they are never to converse with anybody except you and each other. For it is the rare, Euthydemus, that is precious, while water is cheapest, though best, as Pindar said."
>
> – Plato[2]

This paradox of value[3] shows something interesting about us humans: we seem to value things on a subjective[4] basis, but do so with certain non-arbitrary criteria. Something might be *precious* to us for a variety of reasons, but things we value do

---

[1] See *Theory of value (economics)* on Wikipedia [102]
[2] Plato, *Euthydemus* [60]
[3] See *Paradox of value* on Wikipedia [96]
[4] See *Subjective theory of value* on Wikipedia [100]

share certain characteristics. If we can copy something very easily, or if it is naturally abundant, we do not value it.

It seems that we value something because it is scarce (gold, diamonds, time), difficult or labor-intensive to produce, can't be replaced (an old photograph of a loved one), is useful in a way in which it enables us to do things which we otherwise couldn't, or a combination of those, such as great works of art.

Bitcoin is all of the above: it is extremely rare (21 million), increasingly hard to produce (reward halvening), can't be replaced (a lost private key is lost forever), and enables us to do some quite useful things. It is arguably the best tool for value transfer across borders, virtually resistant to censorship and confiscation in the process, plus, it is a self-sovereign store of value, allowing individuals to store their wealth independent of banks and governments, just to name two.

Bitcoin taught me that value is subjective but not arbitrary.

11. Money

> *"In my youth, ...*
> *I kept all my limbs very supple,*
> *By the use of this ointment,*
> *five shillings the box –*
> *Allow me to sell you a couple."*
>
> — The Sage

What is money? We use it every day, yet this question is surprisingly difficult to answer. We are dependent on it in ways big and small, and if we have too little of it our lives become very difficult. Yet, we seldom think about the thing which supposedly makes the world go round. Bitcoin forced me to answer this question over and over again: What the hell is money?

In our "modern" world, most people will probably think of pieces of paper when they talk about money, even though most of our money is just a number in a bank account. We are already using zeros and ones as our money, so how is Bitcoin different? Bitcoin is different because at its core it is a very different *type* of money than the money we currently use. To understand this, we will have to take a closer look at what money is, how it came to be, and why gold and silver was used for most of commercial history.

Seashells, gold, silver, paper, bitcoin. In the end, **money is whatever people use as money**, no matter its shape and form, or lack thereof.

Money, as an invention, is ingenious. A world without money is insanely complicated: How many fish will buy me new shoes?

How many cows will buy me a house? What if I don't need anything right now but I need to get rid of my soon-to-be rotten apples? You don't need a lot of imagination to realize that a barter economy is maddeningly inefficient.

The great thing about money is that it can be exchanged for *anything else* — that's quite the invention! As Nick Szabo[1] brilliantly summarizes in *Shelling Out: The Origins of Money* [69], we humans have used all kinds of things as money: beads made of rare materials like ivory, shells, or special bones, various kinds of jewelry, and later on rare metals like silver and gold.

> "In this sense, it's more typical of a precious metal. Instead of the supply changing to keep the value the same, the supply is predetermined and the value changes."
>
> – Satoshi Nakamoto[2]

Being the lazy creatures we are, we don't think too much about things which just work. Money, for most of us, works just fine. Like with our cars or our computers, most of us are only forced to think about the inner workings of these things if they break down. People who saw their life-savings vanish because of hyperinflation know the value of hard money, just like people who saw their friends and family vanish because of the atrocities of Nazi Germany or Soviet Russia know the value of privacy.

The thing about money is that it is all-encompassing. Money is half of every transaction, which imbues the ones who are in charge of creating money with enormous power.

---

[1] http://unenumerated.blogspot.com/
[2] Satoshi Nakamoto, in a reply to Sepp Hasslberger [50]

> "Given that money is one half of every commercial transaction and that whole civilizations literally rise and fall based on the quality of their money, we are talking about an awesome power, one that flies under the cover of night. It is the power to weave illusions that appear real as long as they last. That is the very core of the Fed's power."
>
> – Ron Paul[3]

Bitcoin peacefully removes this power, since it does away with money creation and it does so without the use of force.

Money went through multiple iterations. Most iterations were good. They improved our money in one way or another. Very recently, however, the inner workings of our money got corrupted. Today, almost all of our money is simply created *out of thin air* by the powers that be. To understand how this came to be I had to learn about the history and subsequent downfall of money.

If it will take a series of catastrophes or simply a monumental educational effort to correct this corruption remains to be seen. I pray to the gods of sound money that it will be the latter.

Bitcoin taught me what money is.

---

[3]Ron Paul, *End the Fed* [57]

12. The History and Downfall of Money

> *"They would not remember the simple rules their friends had given them, such as, that, if you get into the fire, it will burn you, and that, if you cut your finger very deeply with a knife, it generally bleeds, and she had never forgotten that, if you drink a bottle marked 'poison,' it is almost certain to disagree with you, sooner or later."*
> – Lewis Carroll, *Alice in Wonderland*

Many people think that money is backed by gold, which is locked away in big vaults, protected by thick walls. This ceased to be true many decades ago. I am not sure what I thought, since I was in much deeper trouble, having virtually no understanding of gold, paper money, or why it would need to be backed by something in the first place.

One part of learning about Bitcoin is learning about fiat money: what it means, how it came to be, and why it might not be the best idea we ever had. So, what exactly is fiat money? And how did we end up using it?

If something is imposed by *fiat*, it simply means that it is imposed by formal authorization or proposition. Thus, fiat money is money simply because *someone* says that it is money. Since all governments use fiat currency today, this someone is *your* government. Unfortunately, you are not *free* to disagree with this value proposition. You will quickly feel that this proposition is everything but non-violent. If you refuse to use this paper

Figure 12.1.: fiat — 'Let it be done'

currency to do business and pay taxes the only people you will be able to discuss economics with will be your cellmates.

The value of fiat money does not stem from its inherent properties. How good a certain type of fiat money is, is only correlated to the political and fiscal (in)stability of those who dream it into existence. Its value is imposed by decree, arbitrarily.

Until recently, two types of money were used: **commodity money**, made out of precious *things*, and **representative money**, which simply *represents* the precious thing, mostly in writing.

We already touched on commodity money above. People used special bones, seashells, and precious metals as money. Later on, mainly coins made out of precious metals like gold and silver were used as money. The oldest coin found so far is made of a natural gold-and-silver mix and was made more than 2700 years ago.[1] If something is new in Bitcoin, the concept of a coin is not it.

---

[1] According to the Greek historian Herodotus, writing in the fifth century BC, the Lydians were the first people to have used gold and silver coinage. [47]

Figure 12.2.: Lydian electrum coin. Picture cc-by-sa Classical Numismatic Group, Inc.

Turns out that hoarding coins, or hodling, to use today's parlance, is almost as old as coins. The earliest coin hodler was someone who put almost a hundred of these coins in a pot and buried it in the foundations of a temple, only to be found 2500 years later. Pretty good cold storage if you ask me.

One of the downsides of using precious metal coins is that they can be clipped, effectively debasing the value of the coin. New coins can be minted from the clippings, inflating the money supply over time, devaluing every individual coin in the process. People were literally shaving off as much as they could get away with of their silver dollars. I wonder what kind of *Dollar Shave Club* advertisements they had back in the day.

Since governments are only cool with inflation if they are the ones doing it, efforts were made to stop this guerrilla debasement. In classic cops-and-robbers fashion, coin clippers got ever more creative with their techniques, forcing the "masters of the mint" to get even more creative with their countermeasures. Isaac Newton, the world-renowned physicist of *Principia Mathematica* fame, used to be one of these masters. He is attributed with adding the small stripes at the side of coins which are still present today. Gone were the days of easy coin shaving.

Figure 12.3.: Clipped silver coins of varying severity.

Even with these methods of coin debasement[2] kept in check, coins still suffer from other issues. They are bulky and not very convenient to transport, especially when large transfers of value need to happen. Showing up with a huge bag of silver dollars every time you want to buy a Mercedes isn't very practical.

Speaking of German things: How the United States *dollar* got its name is another interesting story. The word "dollar" is derived from the German word *Thaler*, short for a *Joachimsthaler* [101]. A Joachimsthaler was a coin minted in the town of *Sankt Joachimsthal*. Thaler is simply a shorthand for someone (or something) coming from the valley, and because Joachimsthal was *the* valley for silver coin production, people simply referred to these silver coins as *Thaler*. Thaler (German) morphed into daalders (Dutch), and finally dollars (English).

The introduction of representative money heralded the downfall of hard money. Gold certificates were introduced in 1863,

---

[2]Besides clipping, sweating (shaking the coins in a bag and collecting the dust worn off) and plugging (punching a hole in the middle and hammering the coin flat to close the hole) were the most prominent methods of coin debasement. [92]

Figure 12.4.: The original 'dollar'. Saint Joachim is pictured with his robe and wizard hat. Picture cc-by-sa Wikipedia user Berlin-George

and about fifteen years later, the silver dollar was also slowly but surely being replaced by a paper proxy: the silver certificate. [99]

It took about 50 years from the introduction of the first silver certificates until these pieces of paper morphed into something that we would today recognize as one U.S. dollar.

Note that the 1928 U.S. silver dollar in Figure 12.5 still goes by the name of *silver certificate*, indicating that this is indeed simply a document stating that the bearer of this piece of paper is owed a piece of silver. It is interesting to see that the text which indicates this got smaller over time. The trace of "certificate" vanished completely after a while, being replaced by the reassuring statement that these are federal reserve notes.

As mentioned above, the same thing happened to gold. Most of the world was on a bimetallic standard [77], meaning coins were made primarily of gold and silver. Having certificates for gold, redeemable in gold coins, was arguably a technological improvement. Paper is more convenient, lighter, and since it

Figure 12.5.: A 1928 U.S. silver dollar. 'Payable to the bearer on demand.' Picture cc-by-sa National Numismatic Collection at the Smithsonian Institution

can be divided arbitrarily by simply printing a smaller number on it, it is easier to break into smaller units.

To remind the bearers (users) that these certificates were representative for actual gold and silver, they were colored accordingly and stated this clearly on the certificate itself. You can fluently read the writing from top to bottom:

> "This certifies that there have been deposited in the treasury of the United States of America one hundred dollars in gold coin payable to the bearer on demand."

In 1963, the words "PAYABLE TO THE BEARER ON DEMAND" were removed from all newly issued notes. Five years later, the redemption of paper notes for gold and silver ended.

The words hinting on the origins and the idea behind paper money were removed. The golden color disappeared. All that was left was the paper and with it the ability of the government to print as much of it as it wishes.

Figure 12.6.: A 1928 U.S. $100 gold certificate. Picture cc-by-sa National Numismatic Collection, National Museum of American History.

With the abolishment of the gold standard in 1971, this century-long sleight-of-hand was complete. Money became the illusion we all share to this day: fiat money. It is worth something because someone commanding an army and operating jails says it is worth something. As can be clearly read on every dollar note in circulation today, "THIS NOTE IS LEGAL TENDER". In other words: It is valuable because the note says so.

By the way, there is another interesting lesson on today's bank notes, hidden in plain sight. The second line reads that this is legal tender "FOR ALL DEBTS, PUBLIC AND PRIVATE". What might be obvious to economists was surprising to me: All money is debt. My head is still hurting because of it, and I will leave the exploration of the relation of money and debt as an exercise to the reader.

As we have seen, gold and silver were used as money for millennia. Over time, coins made from gold and silver were replaced by paper. Paper slowly became accepted as payment. This accep-

Figure 12.7.: A 2004 series U.S. twenty dollar note used today. 'THIS NOTE IS LEGAL TENDER'

tance created an illusion — the illusion that the paper itself has value. The final move was to completely sever the link between the representation and the actual: abolishing the gold standard and convincing everyone that the paper in itself is precious.

Bitcoin taught me about the history of money and the greatest sleight of hand in the history of economics: fiat currency.

13. Fractional Reserve Insanity

> *Alas! it was too late: she went on growing and growing, and very soon had to kneel down: in another minute there was not room even for this, and she tried the effect of lying down, with one elbow against the door, and the other arm curled round her head. Still she went on growing, and as a last resource she put one arm out of the window, and one foot up the chimney, and said to herself "now I can do no more—what will become of me?"*
> – Lewis Carroll, *Alice in Wonderland*

Value and money aren't trivial topics, especially in today's times. The process of money creation in our banking system is equally non-trivial, and I can't shake the feeling that this is deliberately so. What I have previously only encountered in academia and legal texts seems to be common practice in the financial world as well: nothing is explained in simple terms, not because it is truly complex, but because the truth is hidden behind layers and layers of jargon and *apparent* complexity. "Expansionary monetary policy, quantitative easing, fiscal stimulus to the economy." The audience nods along in agreement, hypnotized by the fancy words.

Fractional reserve banking and quantitative easing are two of those fancy words, obfuscating what is really happening by masking it as complex and difficult to understand. If you would explain them to a five-year-old, the insanity of both will become apparent quickly.

Godfrey Bloom, addressing the European Parliament during a joint debate, said it way better than I ever could:

> "[...] you do not really understand the concept of banking. All the banks are broke. Bank Santander, Deutsche Bank, Royal Bank of Scotland — they're all broke! And why are they broke? It isn't an act of God. It isn't some sort of tsunami. They're broke because we have a system called 'fractional reserve banking' which means that banks can lend money that they don't actually have! It's a criminal scandal and it's been going on for too long. [...] We have counterfeiting — sometimes called quantitative easing — but counterfeiting by any other name. The artificial printing of money which, if any ordinary person did, they'd go to prison for a very long time [...] and until we start sending bankers — and I include central bankers and politicians — to prison for this outrage it will continue."
>
> – Godfrey Bloom[1]

Let me repeat the most important part: banks can lend money that they don't actually have.

Thanks to fractional reserve banking, a bank only has to keep a small *fraction* of every dollar it gets. It's somewhere between 0 and 10%, usually at the lower end, which makes things even worse.

Let's use a concrete example to better understand this crazy idea: A fraction of 10% will do the trick and we should be able to do all the calculations in our head. Win-win. So, if you take $100 to a bank — because you don't want to store it under your mattress — they only have to keep the agreed upon *fraction* of

---

[1] Joint debate on the banking union [17]

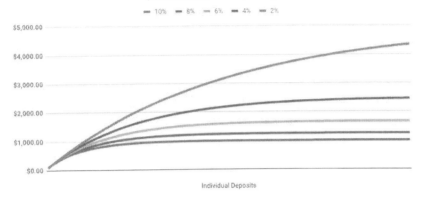

Figure 13.1.: The money multiplier effect

it. In our example that would be $10, because 10% of $100 is $10. Easy, right?

So what do banks do with the rest of the money? What happens to your $90? They do what banks do, they lend it to other people. The result is a money multiplier effect, which increases the money supply in the economy enormously (Figure 13.1). Your initial deposit of $100 will soon turn into $190. By lending a 90% fraction of the newly created $90, there will soon be $271 in the economy. And $343.90 after that. The money supply is recursively increasing, since banks are literally lending money they don't have [93]. Without a single Abracadabra, banks magically transform $100 into one thousand dollars or more. Turns out 10x is easy. It only takes a couple of lending rounds.

Don't get me wrong: There is nothing wrong with lending. There is nothing wrong with interest. There isn't even anything wrong with good old regular banks to store your wealth some-

Figure 13.2.: Yellen is strongly opposed to audit the Fed, while Bitcoin Sign Guy is strongly in favor of buying bitcoin.

where more secure than in your sock drawer.

Central banks, however, are a different beast. Abominations of financial regulation, half public half private, playing god with something which affects everyone who is part of our global civilization, without a conscience, only interested in the immediate future, and seemingly without any accountability or auditability (see Figure 13.2).

While Bitcoin is still inflationary, it will cease to be so rather soon. The strictly limited supply of 21 million bitcoins will eventually do away with inflation completely. We now have two monetary worlds: an inflationary one where money is printed arbitrarily, and the world of Bitcoin, where final supply is fixed and easily auditable for everyone. One is forced upon us by violence, the other can be joined by anyone who wishes to do so. No barriers to entry, no one to ask for permission. Voluntary participation. That is the beauty of Bitcoin.

I would argue that the argument between Keynesian[2] and Austrian[3] economists is no longer purely academical. Satoshi managed to build a system for value transfer on steroids, creating the soundest money which ever existed in the process. One way or another, more and more people will learn about the scam which is fractional reserve banking. If they come to similar conclusions as most Austrians and Bitcoiners, they might join the ever-growing internet of money. Nobody can stop them if they choose to do so.

Bitcoin taught me that fractional reserve banking is pure insanity.

---

[2]Theories according to John Maynard Keynes and his deciples [86]
[3]School of economic thought based on methodological individualism [76]

14. Sound Money

> *"The first thing I've got to do," said Alice to herself, as she wandered about in the wood, "is to grow to my right size, and the second thing is to find my way into that lovely garden. I think that will be the best plan."*
> — Lewis Carroll, *Alice in Wonderland*

The most important lesson I have learned from Bitcoin is that in the long run, hard money is superior to soft money. Hard money, also referred to as *sound money*, is any globally traded currency that serves as a reliable store of value.

Granted, Bitcoin is still young and volatile. Critics will say that it does not store value reliably. The volatility argument is missing the point. Volatility is to be expected. The market will take a while to figure out the just price of this new money. Also, as is often jokingly pointed out, it is grounded in an error of measurement. If you think in dollars you will fail to see that one bitcoin will always be worth one bitcoin.

> "A fixed money supply, or a supply altered only in accord with objective and calculable criteria, is a necessary condition to a meaningful just price of money."
>
> — Fr. Bernard W. Dempsey, S.J.[1]

---
[1] Perry J. Roets, S.J., *Review of Social Economy* [62]

$$\sum_{i=0}^{32} \frac{21000 \lfloor \frac{50*10^8}{2^i} \rfloor}{10^8} \qquad (14.1)$$

Figure 14.1.: Bitcoin's supply formula

As a quick stroll through the graveyard of forgotten currencies has shown, money which can be printed will be printed. So far, no human in history was able to resist this temptation.

Bitcoin does away with the temptation to print money in an ingenious way. Satoshi was aware of our greed and fallibility — this is why he chose something more reliable than human restraint: mathematics.

While this formula is useful to describe Bitcoin's supply, it is actually nowhere to be found in the code. Issuance of new bitcoin is done in an algorithmically controlled fashion, by reducing the reward which is paid to miners every four years [13]. The formula above is used to quickly sum up what is happening under the hood. What really happens can be best seen by looking at the change in block reward, the reward paid out to whoever finds a valid block, which roughly happens every 10 minutes.

Formulas, logarithmic functions and exponentials are not exactly intuitive to understand. The concept of *soundness* might be easier to understand if looked at in another way. Once we know how much there is of something, and once we know how hard this something is to produce or get our hands on, we immediately understand its value. What is true for Picasso's paintings, Elvis Presley's guitars, and Stradivarius violins is also true for fiat currency, gold, and bitcoins.

The hardness of fiat currency depends on who is in charge of the respective printing presses. Some governments might be more willing to print large amounts of currency than others, re-

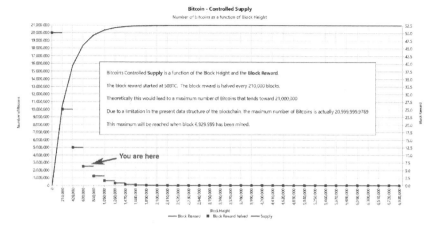

Figure 14.2.: Bitcoin's controlled supply

sulting in a weaker currency. Other governments might be more restrictive in their money printing, resulting in harder currency.

> "One important aspect of this new reality is that institutions like the Fed cannot go bankrupt. They can print any amount of money that they might need for themselves at virtually zero cost."
>
> – Jörg Guido Hülsmann[2]

Before we had fiat currencies, the soundness of money was determined by the natural properties of the stuff which we used as money. The amount of gold on earth is limited by the laws of physics. Gold is rare because supernovae and neutron star collisions are rare. The "flow" of gold is limited because extracting it is quite an effort. Being a heavy element it is mostly buried deep underground.

The abolishment of the gold standard gave way to a new reality: adding new money requires just a drop of ink. In our

---

[2] Jörg Guido Hülsmann, *The Ethics of Money Production* [38]

$$\frac{190,000t}{3,100t} = 61 \qquad (14.2)$$

Figure 14.3.: Stock-to-flow ratio of gold

modern world adding a couple of zeros to the balance of a bank account requires even less effort: flipping a few bits in a bank computer is enough.

The principle outlined above can be expressed more generally as the ratio of "stock" to "flow". Simply put, the *stock* is how much of something is currently there. For our purposes, the stock is a measure of the current money supply. The *flow* is how much there is produced over a period of time (e.g. per year). The key to understanding sound money is in understanding this stock-to-flow ratio.

Calculating the stock-to-flow ratio for fiat currency is difficult, because how much money there is depends on how you look at it. [94] You could count only banknotes and coins (M0), add traveler checks and check deposits (M1), add saving accounts and mutual funds and some other things (M2), and even add certificates of deposit to all of that (M3). Further, how all of this is defined and measured varies from country to country and since the US Federal Reserve stopped publishing [61] numbers for M3, we will have to make do with the M2 monetary supply. I would love to verify these numbers, but I guess we have to trust the fed for now.

Gold, one of the rarest metals on earth, has the highest stock-to-flow ratio. According to the US Geological Survey, a little more than 190,000 tons have been mined. In the last few years, around 3100 tons of gold have been mined per year. [68]

Using these numbers, we can easily calculate the stock-to-flow ratio for gold (see Figure 14.3).

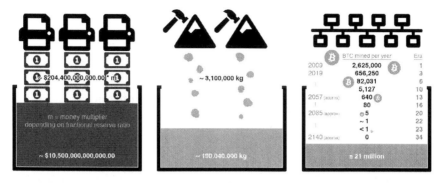

Figure 14.4.: Visualization of stock and flow for USD, gold, and Bitcoin

Nothing has a higher stock-to-flow ratio than gold. This is why gold, up to now, was the hardest, soundest money in existence. It is often said that all the gold mined so far would fit in two olympic-sized swimming pools. According to my calculations[3], we would need four. So maybe this needs updating, or Olympic-sized swimming pools got smaller.

Enter Bitcoin. As you probably know, bitcoin mining was all the rage in the last couple of years. This is because we are still in the early phases of what is called the *reward era*, where mining nodes are rewarded with *a lot* of bitcoin for their computational effort. We are currently in reward era number 3, which began in 2016 and will end in early 2020, probably in May. While the bitcoin supply is predetermined, the inner workings of Bitcoin only allow for approximate dates. Nevertheless, we can predict with certainty how high Bitcoin's stock-to-flow ratio will be. Spoiler alert: it will be high.

How high? Well, it turns out that Bitcoin will get infinitely hard (see Figure 14.4).

---

[3] https://bit.ly/gold-pools

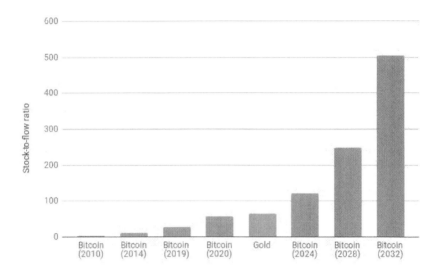

Figure 14.5.: Rising stock-to-flow ratio of bitcoin as compared to gold

Due to an exponential decrease of the mining reward, the flow of new bitcoin will diminish resulting in a sky-rocketing stock-to-flow ratio. It will catch up to gold in 2020, only to surpass it four years later by doubling its soundness again. Such a doubling will occur 64 times in total. Thanks to the power of exponentials, the number of bitcoin mined per year will drop below 100 bitcoin in 50 years and below 1 bitcoin in 75 years. The global faucet which is the block reward will dry up somewhere around the year 2140, effectively stopping the production of bitcoin. This is a long game. If you are reading this, you are still early.

As bitcoin approaches infinite stock to flow ratio it will be the soundest money in existence. Infinite soundness is hard to beat.

Viewed through the lens of economics, Bitcoin's *difficulty adjustment* is probably its most important component. How hard it is to mine bitcoin depends on how quickly new bitcoins are mined.[4] It is the dynamic adjustment of the network's mining difficulty which enables us to predict its future supply.

The simplicity of the difficulty adjustment algorithm might distract from its profundity, but the difficulty adjustment truly is a revolution of Einsteinian proportions. It ensures that, no matter how much or how little effort is spent on mining, Bitcoin's controlled supply won't be disrupted. As opposed to every other resource, no matter how much energy someone will put into mining bitcoin, the total reward will not increase.

Just like $E = mc^2$ dictates the universal speed limit in our universe, Bitcoin's difficulty adjustment dictates the **universal money limit** in Bitcoin.

If it weren't for this difficulty adjustment, all bitcoins would have been mined already. If it weren't for this difficulty adjustment, Bitcoin probably wouldn't have survived in its infancy. It is what secures the network in its reward era. It is what ensures a steady and fair distribution[5] of new bitcoin. It is the thermostat which regulates Bitcoin's monetary policy.

Einstein showed us something novel: no matter how hard you push an object, at a certain point you won't be able to get more speed out of it. Satoshi also showed us something novel: no matter how hard you dig for this digital gold, at a certain point you won't be able to get more bitcoin out of it. For the first time in human history, we have a monetary good which, no matter how hard you try, you won't be able to produce more of.

Bitcoin taught me that sound money is essential.

---

[4] It actually depends on how quickly valid blocks are found, but for our purposes, this is the same thing as "mining bitcoins" and will be so for the next 120 years.

[5] Dan Held, *Bitcoin's Distribution was Fair* [36]

Part III.

Technology

Technology

> *"Now, I'll manage better this time" she said to herself, and began by taking the little golden key, and unlocking the door that led into the garden*
> – Lewis Carroll, *Alice in Wonderland*

Golden keys, clocks which only work by chance, races to solve strange riddles, and builders that don't have faces or names. What sounds like fairy tales from Wonderland is daily business in the world of Bitcoin.

As we explored in Chapter II, large parts of the current financial system are systematically broken. Like Alice, we can only hope to manage better this time. But, thanks to a pseudonymous inventor, we have incredibly sophisticated technology to support us this time around: Bitcoin.

Solving problems in a radically decentralized and adversarial environment requires unique solutions. What would otherwise be trivial problems to solve are everything but in this strange world of nodes. Bitcoin relies on strong cryptography for most solutions, at least if looked at through the lens of technology. Just how strong this cryptography is will be explored in one of the following lessons.

Cryptography is what Bitcoin uses to remove trust in authorities. Instead of relying on centralized institutions, the system relies on the final authority of our universe: physics. Some grains of trust still remain, however. We will examine these grains in the second lesson of this chapter.

Part III – Technology:

15. Strength in numbers

16. Reflections on "Don't Trust, Verify"

17. Telling time takes work

18. Move slowly and don't break things

19. Privacy is not dead

20. Cypherpunks write code

21. Metaphors for Bitcoin's future

The last couple of lessons explore the ethos of technological development in Bitcoin, which is arguably as important as the technology itself. Bitcoin is not the next shiny app on your phone. It is the foundation of a new economic reality, which is why Bitcoin should be treated as nuclear-grade financial software.

Where are we in this financial, societal, and technological revolution? Networks and technologies of the past may serve as metaphors for Bitcoins future, which are explored in the last lesson of this chapter.

Once more, strap in and enjoy the ride. Like all exponential technologies, we are about to go parabolic.

15. Strength in Numbers

> *"Let me see: four times five is twelve, and four times six is thirteen, and four times seven is fourteen—oh dear! I shall never get to twenty at this rate!"*
> – Lewis Carroll, *Alice in Wonderland*

Numbers are an essential part of our everyday life. Large numbers, however, aren't something most of us are too familiar with. The largest numbers we might encounter in everyday life are in the range of millions, billions, or trillions. We might read about millions of people in poverty, billions of dollars spent on bank bailouts, and trillions of national debt. Even though it's hard to make sense of these headlines, we are somewhat comfortable with the size of those numbers.

Although we might seem comfortable with billions and trillions, our intuition already starts to fail with numbers of this magnitude. Do you have an intuition how long you would have to wait for a million/billion/trillion seconds to pass? If you are anything like me, you are lost without actually crunching the numbers.

Let's take a closer look at this example: the difference between each is an increase by three orders of magnitude: 10^6, 10^9, 10^{12}. Thinking about seconds is not very useful, so let's translate this into something we can wrap our head around:

- 10^6: One million seconds was 11/2 weeks ago.

- 10^9: One billion seconds was almost 32 years ago.

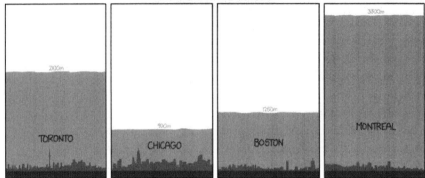

Figure 15.1.: About 1 trillion seconds ago. Source: xkcd 1225

- 10^{12}: One trillion seconds ago Manhattan was covered under a thick layer of ice.[1]

As soon as we enter the beyond-astronomical realm of modern cryptography, our intuition fails catastrophically. Bitcoin is built around large numbers and the virtual impossibility of guessing them. These numbers are way, way larger than anything we might encounter in day-to-day life. Many orders of magnitude larger. Understanding how large these numbers truly are is essential to understanding Bitcoin as a whole.

Let's take SHA-256[2], one of the hash functions[3] used in Bitcoin, as a concrete example. It is only natural to think about 256 bits as "two hundred fifty-six," which isn't a large number at all. However, the number in SHA-256 is talking about orders

---

[1] One trillion seconds (10^{12}) was 31710 years ago. The Last Glacial Maximum was 33,000 years ago. [88]

[2] SHA-256 is part of the SHA-2 family of cryptographic hash functions developed by the NSA. [97]

[3] Bitcoin uses SHA-256 in its block hashing algorithm. [12]

of magnitude — something our brains are not well-equipped to deal with.

While bit length is a convenient metric, the true meaning of 256-bit security is lost in translation. Similar to the millions (10^6) and billions (10^9) above, the number in SHA-256 is about orders of magnitude (2^{256}).

So, how strong is SHA-256, exactly?

> "SHA-256 is very strong. It's not like the incremental step from MD5 to SHA1. It can last several decades unless there's some massive breakthrough attack."
>
> – Satoshi Nakamoto[4]

Let's spell things out. 2^{256} equals the following number:

> 115 quattuorvigintillion 792 trevigintillion 89 duovigintillion 237 unvigintillion 316 vigintillion 195 novemdecillion 423 octodecillion 570 septendecillion 985 sexdecillion 8 quindecillion 687 quattuordecillion 907 tredecillion 853 duodecillion 269 undecillion 984 decillion 665 nonillion 640 octillion 564 septillion 39 sextillion 457 quintillion 584 quadrillion 7 trillion 913 billion 129 million 639 thousand 936.

That's a lot of nonillions! Wrapping your head around this number is pretty much impossible. There is nothing in the physical universe to compare it to. It is far larger than the number of atoms in the observable universe. The human brain simply isn't made to make sense of it.

---

[4]Satoshi Nakamoto, in a reply to questions about SHA-256 collisions. [54]

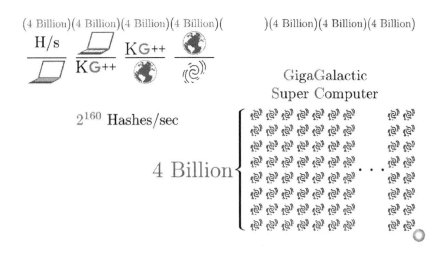

Figure 15.2.: Illustration of SHA-256 security. Original graphic by Grant Sanderson aka 3Blue1Brown.

One of the best visualizations of the true strength of SHA-256 is a video by Grant Sanderson. Aptly named *"How secure is 256 bit security?"*[5] it beautifully shows how large a 256-bit space is. Do yourself a favor and take the five minutes to watch it. As all other *3Blue1Brown* videos it is not only fascinating but also exceptionally well made. Warning: You might fall down a math rabbit hole.

Bruce Schneier [65] used the physical limits of computation to put this number into perspective: even if we could build an optimal computer, which would use any provided energy to flip bits perfectly [87], build a Dyson sphere[6] around our sun, and let it run for 100 billion billion years, we would still only have a 25% chance to find a needle in a 256-bit haystack.

---

[5]Watch the video at https://youtu.be/S9JGmA5_unY

[6]A Dyson sphere is a hypothetical megastructure that completely encompasses a star and captures a large percentage of its power output. [81]

> "These numbers have nothing to do with the technology of the devices; they are the maximums that thermodynamics will allow. And they strongly imply that brute-force attacks against 256-bit keys will be infeasible until computers are built from something other than matter and occupy something other than space."
>
> – Bruce Schneier[7]

It is hard to overstate the profoundness of this. Strong cryptography inverts the power-balance of the physical world we are so used to. Unbreakable things do not exist in the real world. Apply enough force, and you will be able to open any door, box, or treasure chest.

Bitcoin's treasure chest is very different. It is secured by strong cryptography, which does not give way to brute force. And as long as the underlying mathematical assumptions hold, brute force is all we have. Granted, there is also the option of a global $5 wrench attack (Figure 15.3) But torture won't work for all bitcoin addresses, and the cryptographic walls of bitcoin will defeat brute force attacks. Even if you come at it with the force of a thousand suns. Literally.

This fact and its implications were poignantly summarized in the call to cryptographic arms: *"No amount of coercive force will ever solve a math problem."*

> "It isn't obvious that the world had to work this way. But somehow the universe smiles on encryption."
>
> – Julian Assange[8]

---

[7]Bruce Schneier, *Applied Cryptography* [64]
[8]Julian Assange, *A Call to Cryptographic Arms* [5]

Figure 15.3.: $5 wrench attack. Source: xkcd 538

Nobody yet knows for sure if the universe's smile is genuine or not. It is possible that our assumption of mathematical asymmetries is wrong and we find that P actually equals NP [95], or we find surprisingly quick solutions to specific problems [79] which we currently assume to be hard. If that should be the case, cryptography as we know it will cease to exist, and the implications would most likely change the world beyond recognition.

"Vires in Numeris" = "Strength in Numbers"[9]

Vires in numeris is not only a catchy motto used by bitcoiners. The realization that there is an unfathomable strength to be found in numbers is a profound one. Understanding this, and the inversion of existing power balances which it enables changed my view of the world and the future which lies ahead of us.

One direct result of this is the fact that you don't have to ask anyone for permission to participate in Bitcoin. There is no page to sign up, no company in charge, no government agency

---

[9] *Vires in Numeris* was first proposed as a Bitcoin motto by the bitcointalk user *epii* [25]

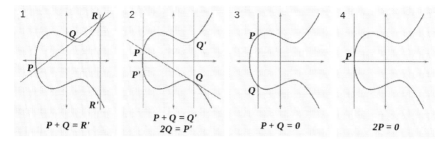

Figure 15.4.: Elliptic curve examples. Graphic cc-by-sa Emmanuel Boutet.

to send application forms to. Simply generate a large number and you are pretty much good to go. The central authority of account creation is mathematics. And God only knows who is in charge of that.

Bitcoin is built upon our best understanding of reality. While there are still many open problems in physics, computer science, and mathematics, we are pretty sure about some things. That there is an asymmetry between finding solutions and validating the correctness of these solutions is one such thing. That computation needs energy is another one. In other words: finding a needle in a haystack is harder than checking if the pointy thing in your hand is indeed a needle or not. And finding the needle takes work.

The vastness of Bitcoin's address space is truly mind-boggling. The number of private keys even more so. It is fascinating how much of our modern world boils down to the improbability of finding a needle in an unfathomably large haystack. I am now more aware of this fact than ever.

Bitcoin taught me that there is strength in numbers.

16. Reflections on "Don't Trust, Verify"

> *"Now for the evidence," said the King, "and then the sentence."*
> – Lewis Carroll, *Alice in Wonderland*

Bitcoin aims to replace, or at least provide an alternative to, conventional currency. Conventional currency is bound to a centralized authority, no matter if we are talking about legal tender like the US dollar or modern monopoly money like Fortnite's V-Bucks. In both examples, you are bound to trust the central authority to issue, manage and circulate your money. Bitcoin unties this bound, and the main issue Bitcoin solves is the issue of *trust*.

> "The root problem with conventional currency is all the trust that's required to make it work. [...] What is needed is an electronic payment system based on cryptographic proof instead of trust"
>
> – Satoshi Nakamoto[1]

Bitcoin solves the problem of trust by being completely decentralized, with no central server or trusted parties. Not even trusted *third* parties, but trusted parties, period. When there is no central authority, there simply *is* no-one to trust. Complete decentralization is the innovation. It is the root of Bitcoin's

---

[1] Satoshi Nakamoto, official Bitcoin announcement [51] and whitepaper [48]

resilience, the reason why it is still alive. Decentralization is also why we have mining, nodes, hardware wallets, and yes, the blockchain. The only thing you have to "trust" is that our understanding of mathematics and physics isn't totally off and that the majority of miners act honestly (which they are incentivized to do).

While the regular world operates under the assumption of *"trust, but verify,"* Bitcoin operates under the assumption of *"don't trust, verify."* Satoshi made the importance of removing trust very clear in both the introduction as well as the conclusion of the Bitcoin whitepaper.

> "Conclusion: We have proposed a system for electronic transactions without relying on trust."
>
> – Satoshi Nakamoto[2]

Note that *without relying on trust* is used in a very specific context here. We are talking about trusted third parties, i.e. other entities which you trust to produce, hold, and process your money. It is assumed, for example, that you can trust your computer.

As Ken Thompson showed in his Turing Award lecture, trust is an extremely tricky thing in the computational world. When running a program, you have to trust all kinds of software (and hardware) which, in theory, could alter the program you are trying to run in a malicious way. As Thompson summarized in his *Reflections on Trusting Trust*: "The moral is obvious. You can't trust code that you did not totally create yourself." [70]

Thompson demonstrated that even if you have access to the source code, your compiler — or any other program-handling program or hardware — could be compromised and detecting this backdoor would be very difficult. Thus, in practice, a truly

---

[2]Satoshi Nakamoto, the Bitcoin whitepaper [48]

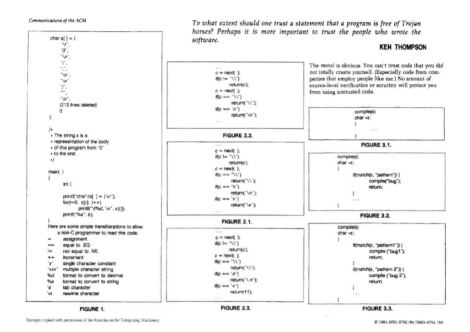

Figure 16.1.: Excerpts from Ken Thompson's paper 'Reflections on Trusting Trust'

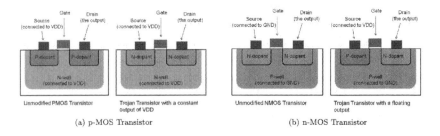

Figure 16.2.: Stealthy Dopant-Level Hardware Trojans by Becker, Regazzoni, Paar, Burleson

trustless system does not exist. You would have to create all your software *and* all your hardware (assemblers, compilers, linkers, etc.) from scratch, without the aid of any external software or software-aided machinery.

> "If you wish to make an apple pie from scratch, you must first invent the universe."
>
> – Carl Sagan[3]

The Ken Thompson Hack is a particularly ingenious and hard-to-detect backdoor, so let's take a quick look at a hard-to-detect backdoor which works without modifying any software. Researchers found a way to compromise security-critical hardware by altering the polarity of silicon impurities. [9] Just by changing the physical properties of the stuff that computer chips are made of they were able to compromise a cryptographically secure random number generator. Since this change can't be seen, the backdoor can't be detected by optical inspection, which is one of the most important tamper-detection mechanism for chips like these.

Sounds scary? Well, even if you would be able to build everything from scratch, you would still have to trust the underlying

---

[3]Carl Sagan, *Cosmos* [63]

mathematics. You would have to trust that *secp256k1* is an elliptic curve without backdoors. Yes, malicious backdoors can be inserted in the mathematical foundations of cryptographic functions and arguably this has already happened at least once. [80] There are good reasons to be paranoid, and the fact that everything from your hardware, to your software, to the elliptic curves used can have backdoors [82] are some of them.

> "Don't trust. Verify."
>
> – Bitcoiners everywhere

The above examples should illustrate that *trustless* computing is utopic. Bitcoin is probably the one system which comes closest to this utopia, but still, it is *trust-minimized* — aiming to remove trust wherever possible. Arguably, the chain-of-trust is neverending, since you will also have to trust that computation requires energy, that P does not equal NP, and that you are actually in base reality and not imprisoned in a simulation by malicious actors.

Developers are working on tools and procedures to minimize any remaining trust even further. For example, Bitcoin developers created Gitian[4], which is a software distribution method to create deterministic builds. The idea is that if multiple developers are able to reproduce identical binaries, the chance of malicious tampering is reduced. Fancy backdoors aren't the only attack vector. Simple blackmail or extortion are real threats as well. As in the main protocol, decentralization is used to minimize trust.

Various efforts are being made to improve upon the chicken-and-egg problem of bootstrapping which Ken Thompson's hack

---

[4]https://gitian.org/

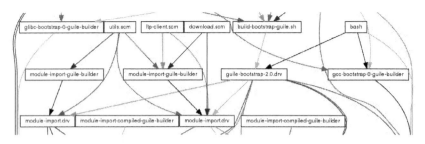

Figure 16.3.: Which came first, the chicken or the egg?

so brilliantly pointed out [20]. One such effort is Guix[5] (pronounced *geeks*), which uses functionally declared package management leading to bit-for-bit reproducible builds by design. The result is that you don't have to trust any software-providing servers anymore since you can verify that the served binary was not tampered with by rebuilding it from scratch. Recently, a pull-request was merged to integrate Guix into the Bitcoin build process.[6]

Luckily, Bitcoin doesn't rely on a single algorithm or piece of hardware. One effect of Bitcoin's radical decentralization is a distributed security model. Although the backdoors described above are not to be taken lightly, it is unlikely that every software wallet, every hardware wallet, every cryptographic library, every node implementation, and every compiler of every language is compromised. Possible, but highly unlikely.

Note that you can generate a private key without relying on any computational hardware or software. You can flip a coin [4] a couple of times, although depending on your coin and tossing style this source of randomness might not be sufficiently random. There is a reason why storage protocols like Glacier[7] advise to

---

[5]https://guix.gnu.org
[6]See PR 15277 of `bitcoin-core`:
  https://github.com/bitcoin/bitcoin/pull/15277
[7]https://glacierprotocol.org/

use casino-grade dice as one of two sources of entropy.

Bitcoin forced me to reflect on what trusting nobody actually entails. It raised my awareness of the bootstrapping problem, and the implicit chain-of-trust in developing and running software. It also raised my awareness of the many ways in which software and hardware can be compromised.

Bitcoin taught me not to trust, but to verify.

17. Telling Time Takes Work

"Dear, dear! I shall be too late!"
— Lewis Carroll, *Alice in Wonderland*

It is often said that bitcoins are mined because thousands of computers work on solving *very complex* mathematical problems. Certain problems are to be solved, and if you compute the right answer, you "produce" a bitcoin. While this simplified view of bitcoin mining might be easier to convey, it does miss the point somewhat. Bitcoins aren't produced or created, and the whole ordeal is not really about solving particular math problems. Also, the math isn't particularly complex. What is complex is *telling the time* in a decentralized system.

As outlined in the whitepaper, the proof-of-work system (aka mining) is a way to implement a distributed timestamp server.

When I first learned how Bitcoin works I also thought that proof-of-work is inefficient and wasteful. After a while, I started to shift my perspective on Bitcoin's energy consumption [29]. It seems that proof-of-work is still widely misunderstood today, in

Figure 17.1.: Excerpts from the whitepaper. Did someone say timechain?

the year 10 AB (after Bitcoin).

Since the problems to be solved in proof-of-work are made up, many people seem to believe that it is *useless* work. If the focus is purely on the computation, this is an understandable conclusion. But Bitcoin isn't about computation. It is about *independently agreeing on the order of things*.

Proof-of-work is a system in which everyone can validate what happened and in what order it happened. This independent validation is what leads to consensus, an individual agreement by multiple parties about who owns what.

In a radically decentralized environment, we don't have the luxury of absolute time. Any clock would introduce a trusted third party, a central point in the system which had to be relied upon and could be attacked. "Timing is the root problem," as Grisha Trubetskoy points out [72]. And Satoshi brilliantly solved this problem by implementing a decentralized clock via a proof-of-work blockchain. Everyone agrees beforehand that the chain with the most cumulative work is the source of truth. It is per definition what actually happened. This agreement is what is now known as Nakamoto consensus.

> "The network timestamps transactions by hashing them into an ongoing chain which serves as proof of the sequence of events witnessed"
>
> – Satoshi Nakamoto[1]

Without a consistent way to tell the time, there is no consistent way to tell before from after. Reliable ordering is impossible. As mentioned above, Nakamoto consensus is Bitcoin's way to consistently tell the time. The system's incentive structure produces a probabilistic, decentralized clock, by utilizing both greed and self-interest of competing participants. The fact that

---

[1] Satoshi Nakamoto, the Bitcoin whitepaper [48]

this clock is imprecise is irrelevant because the order of events is eventually unambiguous and can be verified by anyone.

Thanks to proof-of-work, both the work *and* the validation of the work are radically decentralized. Everyone can join and leave at will, and everyone can validate everything at all times. Not only that, but everyone can validate the state of the system *individually*, without having to rely on anyone else for validation.

Understanding proof-of-work takes time. It is often counterintuitive, and while the rules are simple, they lead to quite complex phenomena. For me, shifting my perspective on mining helped. Useful, not useless. Validation, not computation. Time, not blocks.

Bitcoin taught me that telling the time is tricky, especially if you are decentralized.

18. Move Slowly and Don't Break Things

> *So the boat wound slowly along, beneath the bright summer-day, with its merry crew and its music of voices and laughter...*
> – Lewis Carroll, *Alice in Wonderland*

It might be a dead mantra, but "move fast and break things" is still how much of the tech world operates. The idea that it doesn't matter if you get things right the first time is a basic pillar of the *fail early, fail often* mentality. Success is measured in growth, so as long as you are growing everything is fine. If something doesn't work at first you simply pivot and iterate. In other words: throw enough shit against the wall and see what sticks.

Bitcoin is very different. It is different by design. It is different out of necessity. As Satoshi pointed out, e-currency has been tried many times before, and all previous attempts have failed because there was a head which could be cut off. The novelty of Bitcoin is that it is a beast without heads.

> "A lot of people automatically dismiss e-currency as a lost cause because of all the companies that failed since the 1990's. I hope it's obvious it was only the centrally controlled nature of those systems that doomed them."
>
> – Satoshi Nakamoto[1]

---
[1] Satoshi Nakamoto, in a reply to Sepp Hasslberger [52]

One consequence of this radical decentralization is an inherent resistance to change. "Move fast and break things" does not and will never work on the Bitcoin base layer. Even if it would be desirable, it wouldn't be possible without convincing *everyone* to change their ways. That's distributed consensus. That's the nature of Bitcoin.

> "The nature of Bitcoin is such that once version 0.1 was released, the core design was set in stone for the rest of its lifetime."
>
> – Satoshi Nakamoto[2]

This is one of the many paradoxical properties of Bitcoin. We all came to believe that anything which is software can be changed easily. But the nature of the beast makes changing it bloody hard.

As Hasu beautifully shows in Unpacking Bitcoin's Social Contract [32], changing the rules of Bitcoin is only possible by *proposing* a change, and consequently *convincing* all users of Bitcoin to adopt this change. This makes Bitcoin very resilient to change, even though it is software.

This resilience is one of the most important properties of Bitcoin. Critical software systems have to be antifragile, which is what the interplay of Bitcoin's social layer and its technical layer guarantees. Monetary systems are adversarial by nature, and as we have known for thousands of years solid foundations are essential in an adversarial environment.

> "The rain came down, the floods came, and the winds blew, and beat on that house; and it didn't fall, for it was founded on the rock."
>
> – Matthew 7:24–27

---

[2]Satoshi Nakamoto, in a reply to Gavin Andresen [52]

Arguably, in this parable of the wise and the foolish builders Bitcoin isn't the house. It is the rock. Unchangeable, unmoving, providing the foundation for a new financial system.

Just like geologists, who know that rock formations are always moving and evolving, one can see that Bitcoin is always moving and evolving as well. You just have to know where to look and how to look at it.

The introduction of pay to script hash[3] and segregated witness[4] are proof that Bitcoin's rules can be changed if enough users are convinced that adopting said change is to the benefit of the network. The latter enabled the development of the lightning network[5], which is one of the houses being built on Bitcoin's solid foundation. Future upgrades like Schnorr signatures [59] will enhance efficiency and privacy, as well as scripts (read: smart contracts) which will be indistinguishable from regular transactions thanks to Taproot [31]. Wise builders do indeed build on solid foundations.

Satoshi wasn't only a wise builder technologically. He also understood that it would be necessary to make wise decisions ideologically.

> "Being open source means anyone can independently review the code. If it was closed source, nobody could verify the security. I think it's essential for a program of this nature to be open source."
>
> – Satoshi Nakamoto[6]

---

[3] Pay to script hash (P2SH) transactions were standardised in BIP 16. They allow transactions to be sent to a script hash (address starting with 3) instead of a public key hash (addresses starting with 1). [15]

[4] Segregated Witness (abbreviated as SegWit) is an implemented protocol upgrade intended to provide protection from transaction malleability and increase block capacity. SegWit separates the *witness* from the list of inputs. [16]

[5] https://lightning.network/

[6] Satoshi Nakamoto, in a reply to SmokeTooMuch [53]

Openness is paramount to security and inherent in open source and the free software movement. As Satoshi pointed out, secure protocols and the code which implements them have to be open — there is no security through obscurity. Another benefit is again related to decentralization: code which can be run, studied, modified, copied, and distributed freely ensures that it is spread far and wide.

The radically decentralized nature of Bitcoin is what makes it move slowly and deliberately. A network of nodes, each run by a sovereign individual, is inherently resistant to change — malicious or not. With no way to force updates upon users the only way to introduce changes is by slowly convincing each and every one of those individuals to adopt a change. This non-central process of introducing and deploying changes is what makes the network incredibly resilient to malicious changes. It is also what makes fixing broken things more difficult than in a centralized environment, which is why everyone tries not to break things in the first place.

Bitcoin taught me that moving slowly is one of its features, not a bug.

19. Privacy is Not Dead

> *The players all played at once without waiting for turns, and quarrelled all the while at the tops of their voices, and in a very few minutes the Queen was in a furious passion, and went stamping about and shouting "off with his head!" of "off with her head!" about once in a minute.*
>
> – Lewis Carroll, *Alice in Wonderland*

If pundits are to believed, privacy has been dead since the 80ies[1]. The pseudonymous invention of Bitcoin and other events in recent history show that this is not the case. Privacy is alive, even though it is by no means easy to escape the surveillance state.

Satoshi went through great lengths to cover up his tracks and conceal his identity. Ten years later, it is still unknown if Satoshi Nakamoto was a single person, a group of people, male, female, or a time-traveling AI which bootstrapped itself to take over the world. Conspiracy theories aside, Satoshi chose to identify himself to be a Japanese male, which is why I don't assume but respect his chosen gender and refer to him as *he*.

Whatever his real identity might be, Satoshi was successful in hiding it. He set an encouraging example for everyone who wishes to remain anonymous: it is possible to have privacy online.

---

[1] https://bit.ly/privacy-is-dead

Figure 19.1.: I am not Dorian Nakamoto.

> "Encryption works. Properly implemented strong crypto systems are one of the few things that you can rely on."
>
> – Edward Snowden[2]

Satoshi wasn't the first pseudonymous or anonymous inventor, and he won't be the last. Some have directly imitated this pseudonymous publication style, like Tom Elvis Yedusor of MimbleWimble [71] fame, while others have published advanced mathematical proofs while remaining completely anonymous [3].

It is a strange new world we are living in. A world where identity is optional, contributions are accepted based on merit, and people can collaborate and transact freely. It will take some adjustment to get comfortable with these new paradigms, but I strongly believe that all of this has the potential to change the world for the better.

We should all remember that privacy is a fundamental human right[3]. And as long as people exercise and defend these rights the battle for privacy is far from over.

Bitcoin taught me that privacy is not dead.

---

[2]Edward Snowden, answers to reader questions [66]
[3]Universal Declaration of Human Rights, *Article 12*. [6]

20. Cypherpunks Write Code

> *"I see you're trying to invent something."*
> – Lewis Carroll, *Alice in Wonderland*

Like many great ideas, Bitcoin didn't come out of nowhere. It was made possible by utilizing and combining many innovations and discoveries in mathematics, physics, computer science, and other fields. While undoubtedly a genius, Satoshi wouldn't have been able to invent Bitcoin without the giants on whose shoulders he was standing on.

> "He who only wishes and hopes does not interfere actively with the course of events and with the shaping of his own destiny."
>
> – Ludwig von Mises[1]

One of these giants is Eric Hughes, one of the founders of the cypherpunk movement and author of *A Cypherpunk's Manifesto*. It's hard to imagine that Satoshi wasn't influenced by this manifesto. It speaks of many things which Bitcoin enables and utilizes, such as direct and private transactions, electronic money and cash, anonymous systems, and defending privacy with cryptography and digital signatures.

---

[1] Ludwig von Mises, *Human Action* [74]

"Privacy is necessary for an open society in the electronic age. [...] Since we desire privacy, we must ensure that each party to a transaction have knowledge only of that which is directly necessary for that transaction. [...] Therefore, privacy in an open society requires anonymous transaction systems. Until now, cash has been the primary such system. An anonymous transaction system is not a secret transaction system. [...] We the Cypherpunks are dedicated to building anonymous systems. We are defending our privacy with cryptography, with anonymous mail forwarding systems, with digital signatures, and with electronic money. Cypherpunks write code."

– Eric Hughes[2]

Cypherpunks do not find comfort in hopes and wishes. They actively interfere with the course of events and shape their own destiny. Cypherpunks write code.

Thus, in true cypherpunk fashion, Satoshi sat down and started to write code. Code which took an abstract idea and proved to the world that it actually worked. Code which planted the seed of a new economic reality. Thanks to this code, everyone can verify that this novel system actually works, and every 10 minutes or so Bitcoin proofs to the world that it is still living.

To make sure that his innovation transcends fantasy and becomes reality, Satoshi wrote code to implement his idea before he wrote the whitepaper. He also made sure not to delay[3] any release forever. After all, "there's always going to be one more thing to do."

---

[2] Eric Hughes, A Cypherpunk's Manifesto [37]

[3] "We shouldn't delay forever until every possible feature is done." – Satoshi Nakamoto [55]

```
 23   map<uint256, CBlockIndex*> mapBlockIndex;
 24   const uint256 hashGenesisBlock("0x000000000019d6689c085ae165831e934ff763ae46a2a6c172b3f1b60a8ce26f");
 25   CBlockIndex* pindexGenesisBlock = NULL;
 26   int nBestHeight = -1;
 27   uint256 hashBestChain = 0;
 28   CBlockIndex* pindexBest = NULL;

675   int64 CBlock::GetBlockValue(int64 nFees) const
676   {
677       int64 nSubsidy = 50 * COIN;
678
679       // Subsidy is cut in half every 4 years
680       nSubsidy >>= (nBestHeight / 210000);
681
682       return nSubsidy + nFees;
683   }
684
685   unsigned int GetNextWorkRequired(const CBlockIndex* pindexLast)
686   {
687       const unsigned int nTargetTimespan = 14 * 24 * 60 * 60; // two weeks
688       const unsigned int nTargetSpacing = 10 * 60;
689       const unsigned int nInterval = nTargetTimespan / nTargetSpacing;
690
691       // Genesis block
692       if (pindexLast == NULL)
693           return bnProofOfWorkLimit.GetCompact();
```

Figure 20.1.: Code excerpts from Bitcoin version 0.1

"I had to write all the code before I could convince myself that I could solve every problem, then I wrote the paper."

– Satoshi Nakamoto[4]

In today's world of endless promises and doubtful execution, an exercise in dedicated building was desperately needed. Be deliberate, convince yourself that you can actually solve the problems, and implement the solutions. We should all aim to be a bit more cypherpunk.

Bitcoin taught me that cypherpunks write code.

---

[4]Satoshi Nakamoto, Re: Bitcoin P2P e-cash paper [49]

21. Metaphors for Bitcoin's Future

> *"I know something interesting is sure to happen..."*
>
> – Lewis Carroll, *Alice in Wonderland*

In the last couple of decades, it became apparent that technological innovation does not follow a linear trend. Whether you believe in the technological singularity or not, it is undeniable that progress is exponential in many fields. Not only that, but the rate at which technologies are being adopted is accelerating, and before you know it the bush in the local schoolyard is gone and your kids are using Snapchat instead. Exponential curves have the tendency to slap you in the face way before you see them coming.

Bitcoin is an exponential technology built upon exponential technologies. *Our World in Data*[1] beautifully shows the rising speed of technological adoption, starting in 1903 with the introduction of landlines (see Figure 21.1). Landlines, electricity, computers, the internet, smartphones; all follow exponential trends in price-performance and adoption. Bitcoin does too [22].

Bitcoin has not one but multiple network effects[2], all of which resulting in exponential growth patterns in their respective area: price, users, security, developers, market share, and adoption as global money.

Having survived its infancy, Bitcoin is continuing to grow every day in more aspects than one. Granted, the technology has not reached maturity yet. It might be in its adolescence. But if

---

[1] https://ourworldindata.org/
[2] Trace Mayer, *The Seven Network Effects of Bitcoin* [43]

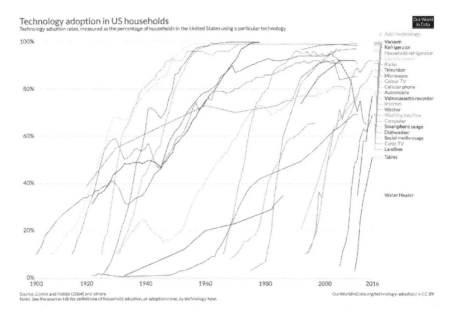

Figure 21.1.: Bitcoin is literally off the charts.

the technology is exponential, the path from obscurity to ubiquity is short.

In his 2003 TED talk, Jeff Bezos chose to use electricity as a metaphor for the web's future.[3] All three phenomena — electricity, the internet, Bitcoin — are *enabling* technologies, networks which enable other things. They are infrastructure to be built upon, foundational in nature.

Electricity has been around for a while now. We take it for granted. The internet is quite a bit younger, but most people already take it for granted as well. Bitcoin is ten years old and has entered public consciousness during the last hype cycle. Only the earliest of adopters take it for granted. As more time passes, more and more people will recognize Bitcoin as something which

---

[3] http://bit.ly/bezos-web

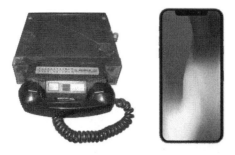

Figure 21.2.: Mobile phone, ca 1965 vs 2019.

simply is.[4]

In 1994, the internet was still confusing and unintuitive. Watching this old recording of the *Today Show*[5] makes it obvious that what feels natural and intuitive now actually wasn't back then. Bitcoin is still confusing and alien to most, but just like the internet is second nature for digital natives, spending and stacking sats[6] will be second nature to the bitcoin natives of the future.

> "The future is already here — it's just not very evenly distributed."
>
> – William Gibson[7]

In 1995, about 15% of American adults used the internet. Historical data from the Pew Research Center [27] shows how the internet has woven itself into all our lives. According to a consumer survey by Kaspersky Lab [40], 13% of respondents have used Bitcoin and its clones to pay for goods in 2018. While

---

[4]This is known as the *Lindy Effect*. The Lindy effect is a theory that the future life expectancy of some non-perishable things like a technology or an idea is proportional to their current age, so that every additional period of survival implies a longer remaining life expectancy. [89]

[5]https://youtu.be/UlJku_CSyNg

[6]https://twitter.com/hashtag/stackingsats

[7]William Gibson, *The Science in Science Fiction* [28]

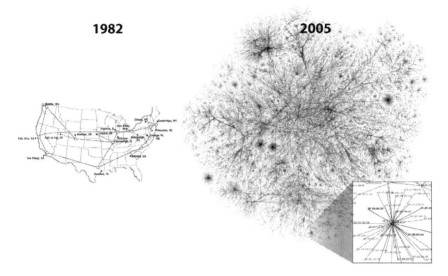

Figure 21.3.: The internet, 1982 vs 2005. Source: cc-by Merit Network, Inc. and Barrett Lyon, Opte Project

payments aren't the only use-case of bitcoin, it is some indication of where we are in Internet time: in the early- to mid-90s.

In 1997, Jeff Bezos stated in a letter to shareholders [11] that "this is Day 1 for the Internet," recognizing the great untapped potential for the internet and, by extension, his company. Whatever day this is for Bitcoin, the vast amounts of untapped potential are clear to all but the most casual observer.

Bitcoin's first node went online in 2009 after Satoshi mined the *genesis block*[8] and released the software into the wild. His

---

[8] The genesis block is the first block of the Bitcoin block chain. Modern versions of Bitcoin number it as block 0, though very early versions counted it as block 1. The genesis block is usually hardcoded into the software of the applications that utilize the Bitcoin block chain. It is a special case in that it does not reference a previous block and produces an unspendable subsidy. The *coinbase* parameter contains, along with the normal data, the following text: *"The Times 03/Jan/2009 Chancellor on brink of second bailout for banks"* [14]

Figure 21.4.: Hal Finney authored the first tweet mentioning bitcoin in January 2009.

node wasn't alone for long. Hal Finney was one of the first people to pick up on the idea and join the network. Ten years later, as of this writing, more than 75.000[9] nodes are running bitcoin.

The protocol's base layer isn't the only thing growing exponentially. The lightning network, a second layer technology, is growing at an even faster rate.

In January 2018, the lightning network had 40 nodes and 60 channels [103]. In April 2019, the network grew to more than 4000 nodes and around 40.000 channels. Keep in mind that this is still experimental technology where loss of funds can and does occur. Yet the trend is clear: thousands of people are reckless and eager to use it.

To me, having lived through the meteoric rise of the web, the parallels between the internet and Bitcoin are obvious. Both are networks, both are exponential technologies, and both enable new possibilities, new industries, new ways of life. Just like electricity was the best metaphor to understand where the internet is heading, the internet might be the best metaphor to understand where bitcoin is heading. Or, in the words of Andreas Antonopoulos, Bitcoin is *The Internet of Money*. These

---

[9]https://bit.ly/luke-nodecount

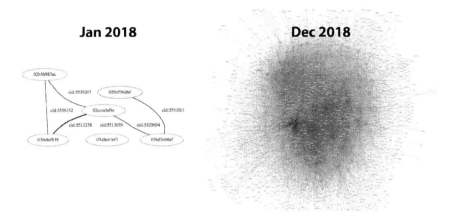

Figure 21.5.: Lightning Network, January 2018 vs December 2018. Source: Jameson Lopp

metaphors are a great reminder that while history doesn't repeat itself, it often rhymes.

Exponential technologies are hard to grasp and often underestimated. Even though I have a great interest in such technologies, I am constantly surprised by the pace of progress and innovation. Watching the Bitcoin ecosystem grow is like watching the rise of the internet in fast-forward. It is exhilarating.

My quest of trying to make sense of Bitcoin has led me down the pathways of history in more ways than one. Understanding ancient societal structures, past monies, and how communication networks evolved were all part of the journey. From the handaxe to the smartphone, technology has undoubtedly changed our world many times over. Networked technologies are especially transformational: writing, roads, electricity, the internet. All of them changed the world. Bitcoin has changed mine and will continue to change the minds and hearts of those who dare to use it.

Bitcoin taught me that understanding the past is essential to understanding its future. A future which is just beginning...

Final Thoughts

Conclusion

> "Begin at the beginning" the King said, very gravely, "and go on till you come to the end: then stop."
> – Lewis Carroll, *Alice in Wonderland*

As mentioned in the beginning, I think that any answer to the question *"What have you learned from Bitcoin?"* will always be incomplete. The symbiosis of what can be seen as multiple living systems – Bitcoin, the technosphere, and economics – is too intertwined, the topics too numerous, and things are moving too fast to ever be fully understood by a single person.

Even without understanding it fully, and even with all its quirks and seeming shortcomings, Bitcoin undoubtedly works. It keeps producing blocks roughly every ten minutes and does so beautifully. The longer Bitcoin continues to work, the more people will opt-in to use it.

> "It's true that things are beautiful when they work. Art is function."
>
> – Giannina Braschi[10]

Bitcoin is a child of the internet. It is growing exponentially, blurring the lines between disciplines. It isn't clear, for example, where the realm of pure technology ends and where another realm begins. Even though Bitcoin requires computers to function efficiently, computer science is not sufficient to understand

---

[10]Giannina Braschi, *Empire of Dreams* [18]

it. Bitcoin is not only borderless in regards to its inner workings but also boundaryless in respect to academic disciplines.

Economics, politics, game theory, monetary history, network theory, finance, cryptography, information theory, censorship, law and regulation, human organization, psychology – all these and more are areas of expertise which might help in the quest of understanding how Bitcoin works and what Bitcoin is.

No single invention is responsible for its success. It is the combination of multiple, previously unrelated pieces, glued together by game theoretical incentives, which make up the revolution that is Bitcoin. The beautiful blend of many disciplines is what makes Satoshi a genius.

Like every complex system, Bitcoin has to make tradeoffs in terms of efficiency, cost, security, and many other properties. Just like there is no perfect solution to deriving a square from a circle, any solution to the problems which Bitcoin tries to solve will always be imperfect as well.

> "I don't believe we shall ever have a good money again before we take the thing out of the hands of government, that is, we can't take it violently out of the hands of government, all we can do is by some sly roundabout way introduce something that they can't stop."
>
> – Friedrich Hayek[11]

Bitcoin is the sly, roundabout way to re-introduce good money to the world. It does so by placing a sovereign individual behind each node, just like Da Vinci tried to solve the intractable problem of squaring a circle by placing the Vitruvian Man in its

---

[11] Friedrich Hayek on Monetary Policy, the Gold Standard, Deficits, Inflation, and John Maynard Keynes https://youtu.be/EYhEDxFwFRU

center. Nodes effectively remove any concept of a center, creating a system which is astonishingly antifragile and extremely hard to shut down. Bitcoin lives, and its heartbeat will probably outlast all of ours.

I hope you have enjoyed these twenty-one lessons. Maybe the most important lesson is that Bitcoin should be examined holistically, from multiple angles, if one would like to have something approximating a complete picture. Just like removing one part from a complex system destroys the whole, examining parts of Bitcoin in isolation seems to taint the understanding of it. If only one person strikes "blockchain" from her vocabulary and replaces it with "a chain of blocks" I will die a happy man.

In any case, my journey continues. I plan to venture further down into the depths of this rabbit hole, and I invite you to tag along for the ride.[12]

---

[12] https://twitter.com/dergigi

Acknowledgments

Thanks to the countless authors and content producers who influenced my thinking on Bitcoin and the topics it touches. There are too many to list them all, but I'll do my best to name a few.

- Thanks to Arjun Balaji for the tweet which motivated me to write this.

- Thanks to Marty Bent for providing endless food for thought and entertainment. If you are not subscribed to Marty's Bent and Tales From The Crypt, you are missing out. Cheers Matt and Marty for guiding us through the rabbit hole.

- Thanks to Michael Goldstein and Pierre Rochard for curating and providing the greatest Bitcoin literature via the Nakamoto Institute. And thank you for creating the Noded Podcast which influenced my philosophical views on Bitcoin substantially.

- Thanks to Saifedean Ammous for his convictions, savage tweets, and writing The Bitcoin Standard

- Thanks to Francis Pouliot for sharing his excitement about finding out about the timechain.

- Thanks to Andreas M. Antonopoulos for all the educational material he has put out over the years.

- Thanks to Peter McCormack for his honest tweets and the What Bitcoin Did podcast, which keeps providing great insights from many areas of the space.

- Thanks to Jannik, Brandon, Matt, Camilo, Daniel, Michael, and Raphael for providing feedback to early drafts of some lessons. Special thanks to Jannik who proofread multiple drafts multiple times.

- Thanks to Dhruv Bansal and Matt Odell for taking the time to discuss some of these ideas with me.

- Thanks to Guy Swann for producing an audio version of 21lessons.com.

- Thanks to Friar Hass for his spiritual support and guidance, and for taking the time to write a foreword for this book.

- Thanks to my wife for putting up with me and my obsessive nature.

- Thanks to my family for supporting me during both the good times and the bad.

- Last but not least, thanks to all the bitcoin maximalists, shitcoin minimalists, shills, bots, and shitposters which reside in the beautiful garden that is Bitcoin twitter.

And finally, thank you for reading this. I hope you enjoyed it as much as I did enjoy writing it.

List of Figures

0.1. Blind monks examining the Bitcoin bull 12

7.1. The Bitcoin rabbit hole is bottomless. 30

9.1. Hyperinflation in the Weimar Republic (1921-1923) 41

12.1. fiat — 'Let it be done' 52
12.2. Lydian electrum coin. Picture cc-by-sa Classical Numismatic Group, Inc. 53
12.3. Clipped silver coins of varying severity. 54
12.4. The original 'dollar'. Saint Joachim is pictured with his robe and wizard hat. Picture cc-by-sa Wikipedia user Berlin-George 55
12.5. A 1928 U.S. silver dollar. 'Payable to the bearer on demand.' Picture cc-by-sa National Numismatic Collection at the Smithsonian Institution . 56
12.6. A 1928 U.S. $100 gold certificate. Picture cc-by-sa National Numismatic Collection, National Museum of American History. 57
12.7. A 2004 series U.S. twenty dollar note used today. 'THIS NOTE IS LEGAL TENDER' 58

13.1. The money multiplier effect 61
13.2. Yellen is strongly opposed to audit the Fed, while Bitcoin Sign Guy is strongly in favor of buying bitcoin................. 62

14.1. Bitcoin's supply formula 66
14.2. Bitcoin's controlled supply 67

14.3. Stock-to-flow ratio of gold 68
14.4. Visualization of stock and flow for USD, gold, and
      Bitcoin 69
14.5. Rising stock-to-flow ratio of bitcoin as compared
      to gold 70

15.1. About 1 trillion seconds ago. Source: xkcd 1225 . 78
15.2. Illustration of SHA-256 security. Original graphic
      by Grant Sanderson aka 3Blue1Brown. 80
15.3. $5 wrench attack. Source: xkcd 538 82
15.4. Elliptic curve examples. Graphic cc-by-sa Emmanuel Boutet. 83

16.1. Excerpts from Ken Thompson's paper 'Reflections on Trusting Trust' 87
16.2. Stealthy Dopant-Level Hardware Trojans by Becker,
      Regazzoni, Paar, Burleson 88
16.3. Which came first, the chicken or the egg? 90

17.1. Excerpts from the whitepaper. Did someone say
      timechain? 93

19.1. I am not Dorian Nakamoto. 102

20.1. Code excerpts from Bitcoin version 0.1 105

21.1. Bitcoin is literally off the charts. 108
21.2. Mobile phone, ca 1965 vs 2019. 109
21.3. The internet, 1982 vs 2005. Source: cc-by Merit
      Network, Inc. and Barrett Lyon, Opte Project . . 110
21.4. Hal Finney authored the first tweet mentioning
      bitcoin in January 2009. 111
21.5. Lightning Network, January 2018 vs December
      2018. Source: Jameson Lopp 112

About the Bibliography

Today, plenty of books have been published about Bitcoin. However, most of the conversation – and thus most of the resources of interest – happen online.

The following bibliography lists books, papers, and online resources alike. If the resource has a URL associated with it, the URL was alive and kicking in October 2019, since I was able to successfully access the resource in question. If any of the following URLs leads to a dead page, I'm sorry. Please let me know[13] so I can update the link(s).

P.S: Bitcoin and IPFS fixes this.

---

[13] https://dergigi.com/contact

Bibliography

[1] Saifedean Ammous. *The Bitcoin Standard: The Decentralized Alternative to Central Banking.* Wiley, 2017.

[2] Saifedean Ammous. Presentation on the bitcoin standard. `https://www.bayernlb.de/internet/media/de/ir/downloads_1/bayernlb_research/sonderpublikationen_1/bitcoin_munich_may_28.pdf`, May 2018.

[3] Jay Pantone Anonymous 4chan Poster, Robin Houston and Vince Vatter. A lower bound on the length of the shortest superpattern. October 2018.

[4] Andreas M Antonopoulos. *Mastering Bitcoin: Programming the Open Blockchain.* " O'Reilly Media, Inc.", 2014.

[5] Julian Assange. Cypherpunks: Freedom and the future of the internet - introduction: A call to cryptographic arms. `https://cryptome.org/2012/12/assange-crypto-arms.htm`, December 2012.

[6] United Nations General Assembly. The universal declaration of human rights, December 1948.

[7] Beautyon. Why america can't regulate bitcoin. `https://hackernoon.com/why-america-cant-regulate-bitcoin-8c77cee8d794`, March 2018.

[8] Beautyon. Bitcoin is. and that is enough. `https://hackernoon.com/`

bitcoin-is-and-that-is-enough-e3116870eed1, October 2019.

[9] Georg T Becker, Francesco Regazzoni, Christof Paar, and Wayne P Burleson. Stealthy dopant-level hardware trojans. In *International Workshop on Cryptographic Hardware and Embedded Systems*, pages 197–214. Springer, 2013.

[10] Marty Bent. Tales from the crypt – a podcast about bitcoin. https://tftc.io/tales-from-the-crypt/, 2017.

[11] Jeff Bezos. To our shareholders. http://media.corporate-ir.net/media_files/irol/97/97664/reports/Shareholderletter97.pdf, 1997.

[12] Bitcoin Wiki contributors. Block hashing algorithm — Bitcoin Wiki. https://en.bitcoin.it/w/index.php?title=Block_hashing_algorithm&oldid=66452, 2019.

[13] Bitcoin Wiki contributors. Controlled supply — Bitcoin Wiki. https://en.bitcoin.it/w/index.php?title=Controlled_supply&oldid=66483, 2019.

[14] Bitcoin Wiki contributors. Genesis block — Bitcoin Wiki. https://en.bitcoin.it/w/index.php?title=Segregated_Witness&oldid=66902, 2019.

[15] Bitcoin Wiki contributors. Pay to script hash — Bitcoin Wiki. https://en.bitcoin.it/w/index.php?title=Pay_to_script_hash&oldid=64705, 2019.

[16] Bitcoin Wiki contributors. Segregated witness — Bitcoin Wiki. https://en.bitcoin.it/w/index.php?title=Segregated_Witness&oldid=66902, 2019.

[17] Godfrey Bloom. Why the whole banking system is a scam. `https://youtu.be/hYzX3YZoMrs`, May 2013.

[18] Giannina Braschi. *Empire of Dreams*. AmazonCrossing, 2011.

[19] Nic Carter. Bitcoin's existential crisis / what is it like to be a bitcoin? `https://medium.com/s/story/what-is-it-like-to-be-a-bitcoin-56109f3e6753`, November 2018.

[20] Guix Contributors. Guix — bootstrapping. `https://guix.gnu.org/manual/en/html_node/Bootstrapping.html`, 2019.

[21] Daniel C Dennett and Douglas R Hofstadter. *The mind's I: fantasies and reflections on self and soul*. Harvester Press, 1981.

[22] Jeff Desjardins. The rising speed of technological adoption. `https://www.visualcapitalist.com/rising-speed-technological-adoption/`, February 2017.

[23] Peter Diamandis. *Abundance : the future is better than you think*. Free Press, New York, 2012.

[24] Dunny. I've learned more about finance, economics, technology, cryptography, human psychology, politics, game theory, legislation, and myself in the last three months of crypto than the last three and a half years of college. `https://twitter.com/BitcoinDunny/status/935330541263519745`, November 2017.

[25] epii. New bitcoin logo. `https://bitcointalk.org/index.php?topic=4994.msg140770#msg140770`, May 2011.

[26] Electronic Frontier Foundation. The crypto wars:governments working to undermine encryption. https://www.eff.org/files/2014/01/03/cryptowarsonepagers-1_cac.pdf, 2018.

[27] Susannah Fox and Lee Rainie. How the internet has woven itself into american life. https://pewrsr.ch/32M7Qmg, February 2014.

[28] William Gibson. The science in science fiction. https://www.npr.org/2018/10/22/1067220/the-science-in-science-fiction, October 2018.

[29] Gigi. Bitcoin's energy consumption – a shift in perspective. https://dergigi.com/2018/06/10/bitcoin-s-energy-consumption/, June 2018.

[30] Gigi. The magic dust of cryptography – how digital information is changing our societybitcoin's gravity. https://dergigi.com/2018/08/17/the-magic-dust-of-cryptography/, Aug 2018.

[31] Gregory Maxwell. Taproot: Privacy preserving switchable scripting. https://lists.linuxfoundation.org/pipermail/bitcoin-dev/2018-January/015614.html, 2018.

[32] Hasu. Unpacking bitcoin's social contract. https://uncommoncore.co/unpacking-bitcoins-social-contract, December 2018.

[33] Friedrich August Hayek. *1980s Unemployment and the Unions: Essays on the Impotent Price Structure of Britain and Monopoly in the Labour Market*. Institute of Economic Affairs, 1984.

[34] Friedrich August Hayek. *The Collected Works of F.A. Hayek, Volume 6, Good Money, Part II.* Routledge, 1999.

[35] Henry Hazlitt. *Economics in One Lesson.* Ludwig von Mises Institute, https://mises.org/library/economics-one-lesson, 1946.

[36] Dan Held. Bitcoin's distribution was fair. https://blog.picks.co/bitcoins-distribution-was-fair-e2ef7bbbc892, 2018.

[37] Eric Hughes. A cypherpunk's manifesto. https://www.activism.net/cypherpunk/manifesto.html, March 1993.

[38] Guido Jörg Hülsmann. *Ethics of Money Production.* Ludwig von Mises Institute, https://mises.org/library/ethics-money-production, 2008.

[39] Robert Kiyosaki. Why the rich are getting richer. https://youtu.be/abMQhaMdQu0, July 2016.

[40] Kaspersky Lab. From festive fun to password panic: Managing money online this christmas. https://www.kaspersky.com/blog/money-report-2018/, 2018.

[41] Jameson Lopp. No one has found the bottom of the bitcoin rabbit hole. https://twitter.com/lopp/status/1061415918616698881, November 2018.

[42] Margo Rapport. History shows price of an ounce of gold equals price of a decent men's suit, says sionna investment managers. https://www.businesswire.com/news/home/20110819005774/en/History-Shows-Price-Ounce-Gold-Equals-Price, 2011.

[43] Trace Mayer. The 7 network effects of bitcoin. https://www.thrivenotes.com/the-7-network-effects-of-bitcoin/, January 2016.

[44] Ralph C. Merkle. Daos, democracy and governance. https://alcor.org/cryonics/Cryonics2016-4.pdf#page=28, July-August 2016.

[45] Fiat Minimalist. Isn't it ironic that bitcoin has taught me more about money than all these years i've spent working for financial institutions? https://twitter.com/fiatminimalist/status/1072880815661436928, December 2018.

[46] The Austrian Mint. Gold: The extraordinary metal. https://www.muenzeoesterreich.at/eng/discover/for-investors/gold-the-extraordinary-metal, November 2017.

[47] British Museum. The origins of coinage. https://www.britishmuseum.org/explore/themes/money/the_origins_of_coinage.aspx, 2007.

[48] Satoshi Nakamoto. Bitcoin: A peer-to-peer electronic cash system. October 2008.

[49] Satoshi Nakamoto. Re: Bitcoin p2p e-cash paper. https://www.metzdowd.com/pipermail/cryptography/2008-November/014832.html, November 2008.

[50] Satoshi Nakamoto. Bitcoin open source implementation of p2p currency. http://p2pfoundation.ning.com/forum/topics/bitcoin-open-source?commentId=2003008%3AComment%3A9562, February 2009.

[51] Satoshi Nakamoto. Bitcoin open source implementation of p2p currency. `http://p2pfoundation.ning.com/forum/topics/bitcoin-open-source`, February 2009.

[52] Satoshi Nakamoto. Re: Bitcoin open source implementation of p2p currency. `http://p2pfoundation.ning.com/forum/topics/bitcoin-open-source`, February 2009.

[53] Satoshi Nakamoto. Re: Questions about bitcoin. `https://bitcointalk.org/index.php?topic=13.msg46#msg46`, December 2009.

[54] Satoshi Nakamoto. Dealing with sha-256 collisions. `https://bitcointalk.org/index.php?topic=191.msg1585#msg1585`, June 2010.

[55] Satoshi Nakamoto. Re: 0.3 almost ready. `https://bitcointalk.org/index.php?topic=199.msg1670#msg1670`, June 2010.

[56] Satoshi Nakamoto. Re: Transactions and scripts: Dup hash160 ... equalverify checksig. `https://bitcointalk.org/index.php?topic=195.msg1611#msg1611`, June 2010.

[57] Ron Paul. *End the Fed*. Grand Central Publishing, `http://endthefed.org/books/`, 2009.

[58] Jordan Pearson. Inside the world of the bitcoin carnivores: Why a small community of bitcoin users is eating meat exclusively. `https://motherboard.vice.com/en_us/article/ne74nw/inside-the-world-of-the-bitcoin-carnivores`, September 2017.

[59] Pieter Wuille. Schnorr signatures for secp256k1. `https://github.com/sipa/bips/blob/bip-schnorr/bip-schnorr.mediawiki`, 2019.

[60] Plato. *Plato in Twelve Volumes, Vol. 3. (Euthydemus section 304a/304b)*. Harvard University Press, `http://www.perseus.tufts.edu/hopper/text?doc=Perseus%3Atext%3A1999.01.0178%3Atext%3DEuthyd.%3Asection%3D304a`, 2017.

[61] Federal Reserve. Money stock measures – discontinuance of m3. `https://www.federalreserve.gov/Releases/h6/discm3.htm`, 2005.

[62] Perry J. Roets. Bernard w. dempsey, s.j. *Review of Social Economy*, 49(4):546–558, 1991.

[63] Carl Sagan. *Cosmos*. Random House, 1980.

[64] Bruce Schneier. *Applied Cryptography: Protocols, Algorithms and Source Code in C*. John Wiley and Sons, 2017.

[65] Bruce Schneier. Schneier on security. `https://www.schneier.com`, 2019.

[66] Edward Snowden. Edward snowden: Nsa whistleblower answers reader questions. `https://www.theguardian.com/world/2013/jun/17/edward-snowden-nsa-files-whistleblower`, June 2013.

[67] Jimmy Song. Why bitcoin is different. `https://medium.com/@jimmysong/why-bitcoin-is-different-e17b813fd947`, April 2018.

[68] U.S. Geological Survey. National minerals information center – mineral commodity summaries. https://www.usgs.gov/centers/nmic/mineral-commodity-summaries, 2019.

[69] Nick Szabo. Shelling out: The origins of money. https://nakamotoinstitute.org/shelling-out/, 2002.

[70] K. Thompson. Reflections on trusting trust. In *ACM Turing award lectures*, page 1983, 2007.

[71] Tom Elvis Jedusor. Mimblewimble origin. https://github.com/mimblewimble/docs/wiki/MimbleWimble-Origin, 2016.

[72] Grisha Trubetskoy. Blockchain proof-of-work is a decentralized clock. https://grisha.org/blog/2018/01/23/explaining-proof-of-work/, 2018.

[73] Peter Van Valkenburgh. Coin center's peter van valkenburg on preserving the freedom to innovate with public blockchains. http://bit.ly/valkenburgh, November 2018.

[74] Ludwig von Mises. *Human Action*. Ludwig von Mises Institute, https://mises.org/library/human-action-0/html/p/607, 1949.

[75] Wikipedia contributors. 2013–present economic crisis in venezuela — Wikipedia, the free encyclopedia. https://en.wikipedia.org/w/index.php?title=2013%E2%80%93present_economic_crisis_in_Venezuela&oldid=918242758, 2019.

[76] Wikipedia contributors. Austrian school — Wikipedia, the free encyclopedia. https://en.wikipedia.org/w/

index.php?title=Austrian_School&oldid=920008469, 2019.

[77] Wikipedia contributors. Bimetallism — Wikipedia, the free encyclopedia. https://en.wikipedia.org/w/index.php?title=Bimetallism&oldid=920537299, 2019.

[78] Wikipedia contributors. Crypto wars — Wikipedia, the free encyclopedia. https://en.wikipedia.org/w/index.php?title=Crypto_Wars&oldid=916147143, 2019.

[79] Wikipedia contributors. Discrete logarithm — Wikipedia, the free encyclopedia. https://en.wikipedia.org/w/index.php?title=Discrete_logarithm&oldid=909625575, 2019.

[80] Wikipedia contributors. Dual ec drbg — Wikipedia, the free encyclopedia. https://en.wikipedia.org/w/index.php?title=Dual_EC_DRBG&oldid=918490393, 2019.

[81] Wikipedia contributors. Dyson sphere — Wikipedia, the free encyclopedia. https://en.wikipedia.org/w/index.php?title=Dyson_sphere&oldid=916621053, 2019.

[82] Wikipedia contributors. Elliptic-curve cryptography — Wikipedia, the free encyclopedia. https://en.wikipedia.org/w/index.php?title=Elliptic-curve_cryptography&oldid=916608234#Backdoors, 2019.

[83] Wikipedia contributors. Hyperinflation — Wikipedia, the free encyclopedia. https://en.wikipedia.org/w/

index.php?title=Hyperinflation&oldid=919343724, 2019.

[84] Wikipedia contributors. Illegal number — Wikipedia, the free encyclopedia. https://en.wikipedia.org/w/index.php?title=Illegal_number&oldid=918772989, 2019.

[85] Wikipedia contributors. Illegal prime — Wikipedia, the free encyclopedia. https://en.wikipedia.org/w/index.php?title=Illegal_prime&oldid=913087454, 2019.

[86] Wikipedia contributors. Keynesian economics — Wikipedia, the free encyclopedia. https://en.wikipedia.org/w/index.php?title=Keynesian_economics&oldid=919881690, 2019.

[87] Wikipedia contributors. Landauer's principle — Wikipedia, the free encyclopedia. https://en.wikipedia.org/w/index.php?title=Landauer%27s_principle&oldid=907333330, 2019.

[88] Wikipedia contributors. Last glacial maximum — Wikipedia, the free encyclopedia. https://en.wikipedia.org/w/index.php?title=Last_Glacial_Maximum&oldid=919510280, 2019.

[89] Wikipedia contributors. Lindy effect — Wikipedia, the free encyclopedia. https://en.wikipedia.org/w/index.php?title=Lindy_effect&oldid=921214819, 2019.

[90] Wikipedia contributors. List of currencies — Wikipedia, the free encyclopedia. https://en.wikipedia.org/

w/index.php?title=List_of_currencies&oldid=897955050, 2019.

[91] Wikipedia contributors. List of historical currencies — Wikipedia, the free encyclopedia. https://en.wikipedia.org/w/index.php?title=List_of_historical_currencies&oldid=919919705, 2019.

[92] Wikipedia contributors. Methods of coin debasement — Wikipedia, the free encyclopedia. https://en.wikipedia.org/w/index.php?title=Methods_of_coin_debasement&oldid=917940627, 2019.

[93] Wikipedia contributors. Money multiplier — Wikipedia, the free encyclopedia. https://en.wikipedia.org/w/index.php?title=Money_multiplier&oldid=918027413, 2019.

[94] Wikipedia contributors. Money supply — Wikipedia, the free encyclopedia. https://en.wikipedia.org/w/index.php?title=Money_supply&oldid=921152289, 2019.

[95] Wikipedia contributors. P versus np problem — Wikipedia, the free encyclopedia. https://en.wikipedia.org/w/index.php?title=P_versus_NP_problem&oldid=919882161, 2019.

[96] Wikipedia contributors. Paradox of value — Wikipedia, the free encyclopedia. https://en.wikipedia.org/w/index.php?title=Paradox_of_value&oldid=906068208, 2019.

[97] Wikipedia contributors. Sha-2 — Wikipedia, the free encyclopedia. https://en.wikipedia.org/w/index.php?title=SHA-2&oldid=917408454, 2019.

[98] Wikipedia contributors. Ship of theseus — Wikipedia, the free encyclopedia. https://en.wikipedia.org/w/index.php?title=Ship_of_Theseus&oldid=923020256, 2019.

[99] Wikipedia contributors. Silver certificate (united states) — Wikipedia, the free encyclopedia. https://en.wikipedia.org/w/index.php?title=Silver_certificate_(United_States)&oldid=917688197, 2019.

[100] Wikipedia contributors. Subjective theory of value — Wikipedia, the free encyclopedia. https://en.wikipedia.org/w/index.php?title=Subjective_theory_of_value&oldid=893004286, 2019.

[101] Wikipedia contributors. Thaler — Wikipedia, the free encyclopedia. https://en.wikipedia.org/w/index.php?title=Thaler&oldid=914457345, 2019.

[102] Wikipedia contributors. Theory of value (economics) — Wikipedia, the free encyclopedia. https://en.wikipedia.org/w/index.php?title=Theory_of_value_(economics)&oldid=919603374, 2019.

[103] Wilma Woo. 'unfairly cheap' lightning network mainnet hits 40 nodes, 60 channels. https://bitcoinist.com/bitcoin-lightning-network-mainnet-nodes/, January 2018.

Printed in Great Britain
by Amazon